AMONG THE GNOMES

An Occult Tale of Adventure in theUntersberg

Nadakkavu, Kozhikode, Kerala, 673011
www.insightpublica.com
e-mail: insightpublica@gmail.com
Title: **AMONG THE GNOMES An Occult Tale of Adventure in the Untersberg**
Author: **FRANZ HARTMANN, M.D.**
First Insight Edition: August 2024
Copyright © Reserved
All rights reserved.
Printed and Published by
InsightinPublica Printers & Publishers Pvt. Ltd.
ISBN: 978-93-5517-790-2
₹210

AMONG THE GNOMES:

An Occult Tale of Adventure in the Untersberg

FRANZ HARTMANN, M.D.

Contents

I

INTRODUCTION 7

II

IN THE DRAGON'S DEN 19

III

WITHIN THE UNTERSBERG 38

IV

AMONG THE GNOMES................................... 62

V

AMONG THE GNOMES................................... 74

VI

LUCIFER 89

VII

DIGGING FOR LIGHT......................................107

VIII

WAR 123

I
INTRODUCTION

THE HAUNTED CASTLE

WHO has ever occupied himself seriously with the investigation of the "night-side of Nature," or studied the works of Theophrastus Paracelsus, and not become acquainted with the celebrated "Untersberg" (the "mountain of the lower world") and its mysterious inhabitants, the fairies and gnomes?

Like a gigantic outpost of the Austrian Alps, this snow-capped wing of the mountains stands on the frontier of Germany, overlooking the Bavarian plains, dotted with hills, forests, and lakes. Its summit, dwelling above the clouds, dominates the valley through which the Salzach river winds its way to the Inn and the Danube. Seen from the north side, where the city of Salzburg is nestled among the hills, the mountain looks tame enough, rising in undulating forest-covered lines up to a height of some seven thousand feet; but on the south side it exhibits an almost endless variety of perpendicular walls, formed of marble rocks thousands of feet high, and interrupted by deep ravines and chasms, craggy cliffs, spurs, and precipices, over which in the time of spring, when the snow begins to melt, great avalanches come thundering down, and a sharp eye may detect in many an inaccessible spot mysterious caves, that seem to penetrate into the bowels of that mysterious mountain. If you will take the trouble of climbing up to these dizzy heights, you will find yourself in a new world, for there the Untersberg appears not as one single mountain, but as a mountain chain, of which each separate link has its special aspect and character, being separated from its neighbour by deep chasms, through which the mountain streams rush. There is no end of waterfalls, caves and labyrinths of boulders, where the inexperienced wanderer may lose his way, especially if he is misled by the gnomes—which may easily occur if his intentions are not pure.

The Untersberg is known to be inhabited by certain kinds of elemental spirits of Nature, some of which are good and benevolent, others of a wicked and malicious nature, and inimical to mankind; and there are innumerable tales circulating among the people in the neighbourhood, telling about the doings of the gnomes, fairies, wild women, and giants, dwelling within caves and in gorgeous marble halls and grottoes filled with gold and precious stones that will turn into dead leaves and stones when seen in the light of day. Some of the friendly tribes come out of the Untersberg on certain occasions, and they are said to have sometimes associated with the inhabitants of our plane of existence, partaking in the dances and amusements of the peasants, and even taking stray children with them into the Untersberg; and, incredible as it may appear, it is even asserted by "those who know" that marriages have taken place between citizens of our world and the inhabitants of the kingdom of gnomes, and that these spirits of Nature, being themselves not immortal, seek to obtain immortality by their union with immortal man. The majority of the gnomes, therefore, also love plain, truthful, and unsophisticated human beings, such as possess a soul in which the light of the immortal spirit may be perceived, and with these they are ready to associate; but with soulless

     The comet-drivers

beings, such as sophisticated, sceptical, arrogant, short-sighted and opinionated scientists, whose hearts are dead, and whose brains are swollen with the products of their own fancy, they will have nothing to do; to such they never show themselves, but love to play tricks upon them whenever they come with a view of invading their kingdom.

Of course it is known to everybody that within the mysterious depths of the Untersberg there dwells the soul of a great emperor in his astral form. There, together with his retinue, he sleeps an enchanted sleep, waiting for the liberation of his country. Sometimes very suddenly, even on a clear summer day, clouds are seen to issue from the sides of the mountain; grotesquely-formed ghost-like mists arise from caverns and precipices, crawling and gliding slowly upwards toward the top, and from the neighbouring peaks also clouds of monstrous shapes and sometimes of gigantic proportions come floating on, until the head of the Untersberg is surrounded by a surging sea of vapours growing dense and dark. Then a clap of thunder reverberates through the rocks, awakening hundreds of echoes, and forked streaks of lightning flash down into the valley; the storm-king arises, howling dismally through the forest, breaking down old trees and hurling them into the precipices below. On such occasions the people in the valleys piously make the sign of the cross, and whisper to each other: "The great emperor has awakened and is reviewing his troops. He is angry because he sees that the black ravens are still flying around the top of the Untersberg." This, of course, I hold to be a fable, and the "emperor in the Untersberg" is well known to the wise; but as to the dark birds referred to, they are typified by certain black-robed and stiff-necked gentlemen, whom you may frequently meet. The liberation for which the emperor waits also seems to me not that from any foreign yoke, but the redemption from selfishness with its consequent evils. Poor emperor! You may have to wait still another thousand years in the world of the gnomes before you will be able to resume control over your kingdom. Sleep in peace! The time will not seem to you long; for it is not you who suffers, and there is no measurement of time during sleep or in eternity.

Owing to the increase of modern culture, and its accompanying sophistry and scepticism, visible intercourse with the gnomes has become of comparatively rare occurrence, especially because their kindness has often been abused and their services misapplied, as the following story will show, which I may be permitted to insert, as it is not without bearing upon the events told in the succeeding chapters.

A short distance from the city of Salzburg, and upon a hill covered by a forest of pines, there stood in ancient times the castle of Tollenstein, of which now only some remnants are left. The walls are in ruins, but these go to show that formerly they were parts of a palatial building. One remnant composed of huge square stones still indicates the extent of the large banqueting-hall, where festivals took place; and it is said that on certain nights the orgies which these stones witnessed are spectrally repeated and enacted in the astral light by the ghost-like shapes of deceased ladies and knights; while not far off there is a dilapidated tower of massive structure, enclosing a deep hole in the ground, where the subterranean dungeon was located—the "oubliette" or living tomb, in which poor wretches for some offence were buried alive and "forgotten," left to starve or suffocate. It is said that, during the nights when the ghosts in the banqueting-hall hold gruesome carousals, cries and groans and wails may be heard coming from the bottom of that well. These things I do not find difficult to believe; for we often find similar instances of the proximity of luxury and misery among the living in this our material world.

In ancient times the owner of the castle was Burkhart von Tollenstein, a youthful and valorous knight, admired by all the ladies in the country on account of the voluminous mass of golden hair which adorned his head. This, together with his manliness and beauty, gained for him the hearts of all those fair ladies, except one, and this was the very one for whose possession he craved, namely, the very beautiful but proud Julia von Horst.

He had seen her only once, but that was enough to make him fall desperately in love with her face and figure. He had been happy enough until he was so unfortunate as to have the tranquillity of his heart destroyed by the sight of her dark and languishing eyes. From that time forward an image of the beautiful Julia was formed in his mind, whose contemplation absorbed him so that he thought of nothing else; henceforth nothing but the thought of Julia had any attraction for him. He sought to woo and to win the ideal of his thoughts; but alas! his sighs and tears were all in vain, for his home was poor, and the proud Julia cared far more for money than for love! She knew that Burkhart's fortune was too small to supply her with all the luxuries she desired; therefore, when he offered her his heart, she rejected it, and sneeringly said:

"Of what use will be your heart to me, if starvation waits for me in your home?"

This offensive remark was more than a knight of these times was able to bear in patience, and Burkhart, cursing his poverty, went home in despair. From day to day he became more and more morose and melancholy, grieving on account of the insufficiency of his means. At last he determined to enrich himself by whatever means he might find, and resolved to rob the gnomes of the Untersberg of their treasures.

In these times it was customary for almost everybody to have a wise and faithful steward ready to give good advice. Burkhart's steward did his best to dissuade the knight from this wicked and dangerous undertaking; but in vain did old Bruno, for this was his name, entreat him to desist from evil thoughts, and to forget the proud Julia, as she was entirely unworthy of his affection. The knight would not listen.

"The Lord be merciful to you!" exclaimed Bruno. "Shake off this delusion, O noble knight; think of your high descent and what your ancestors would say. Look upwards, to where your salvation rests; the spirits of the lower world will mislead and ruin you."

But the knight answered, "I am not a coward. I am not afraid of losing my life, which is worthless to me without the possession of Julia. More than once I have looked into the face of death while engaged in battle. I want the gold of the gnomes, and must have it, let the consequences be what they may. If the gnomes are not willing to surrender their gold, I shall take it by force."

Thus spurning good advice, the knight gave orders that his black war-horse be brought forth. This he bestrode, and trotted towards the Untersberg.

It was a gloomy evening in November; the leaves of the trees had turned yellow and red, and rustled in the wind, and their voices seemed to warn him not to proceed, while the waving boughs motioned to him to return. Soon the queen of the night began to spread her mantle over the face of the earth, and there arose in the gloom, like a gigantic shadow, the outlines of the mysterious Untersberg. For a moment fear overcame the youth, and he stopped; but his desire overcame his fear, and pronouncing an oath he spurred his horse, determined to push on. Just then the horse shied, and, looking up, Burkhart saw sitting by the roadside a dwarf clothed in a steel-blue gown. The dwarf looked steadily with glittering eyes at the knight.

"Avaunt!" exclaimed Burkhart angrily. "What are you sitting here and frightening my horse for?"

"Ho! ho!" laughed the dwarf. "Know, you creeping worm of the earth, I am Pypo, the king of the gnomes. Mine is the Untersberg with its treasures. What have you to seek in my territory?"

When Burkhart heard these words he deemed it prudent to speak politely to the king of the gnomes. He therefore explained to him his situation, and asked for the loan of a sum of money, for which he promised his everlasting gratitude.

The king groaned. "Confound your gratitude," he said; "there would be plenty of wretches like you coming to borrow money from me, if it could be had at such a cheap price."

"What then do you demand?" asked the knight. "State your terms, and I will accept them, for I must have gold at any price!"

"Listen then," said the gnome; "it is not much that I ask. Only one hair from your head for each thousand of florins." Thus saying, his eyes rested searchingly upon the face of the knight.

"Only one hair from my head?" exclaimed Burkhart in great astonishment. "A whole lot of hair you shall have, and be welcome, if you only furnish me the money necessary for obtaining the favour of Julia."

"I am putting no limits to the amount you may draw," laughed the king. "For each thousand of florins which you receive from me you will have to leave me one hair from your head."

"It is a bargain!" exclaimed the knight joyfully, and, drawing his dagger, he was about to proceed to cut a lock of hair from his forehead to offer it to the king.

"Not so," said Pypo. "Only one hair at a time, and I will have to pull it out myself by the root."

So the knight dismounted, and as he bent down the dwarf tore a single hair from his scalp, after which he threw a bag of gold at Burkhart's feet.

"Thanks!" exclaimed the knight, as he hugged the bag and gloated over its contents.

"No thanks are wanted," replied the gnome; "see to it that the hairs upon your head will not become too few in time to purchase enough gold for satisfying the greed of your Julia."

So saying the gnome vanished; but the knight returned with his bag of gold to the castle. He now at once began to enlarge and improve his house in exquisite style; he bought costly furniture and ornaments, hired servants and cooks, sent out invitations for dinners and balls, and every evening he went to the Untersberg for another bag of gold, leaving in return one of his hairs.

Soon the news of the riches of Burkhart von Tollenstein began to spread, and everybody wondered and came to see and admire the luxury displayed by the knight. Now the consent of Julia was easily gained, and before many days the walls of the castle resounded with gay music, merry-making, and laughter; for the marriage of the valorous knight with the beautiful countess took place. All the nobility in the country were invited, and took part in the revel.

Henceforth the castle of Tollenstein became the scene of an uninterrupted succession of festivities of all kinds; there was a merry-go-round, and the doors of the house were open day and night to visitors. Parasites of all kinds peopled the castle. Dinners, dances, masquerades, tournaments, theatrical performances and hunting excursions followed each other without end, and the beautiful Julia had the sweet satisfaction of being surrounded by flatterers and admirers to her heart's content; but her desires grew in proportion as they were gratified, her vanity in proportion as it was tickled: her whims were incalculable, but the resources of her husband seemed to be inexhaustible, and he was an object of envy to everyone.

More and more frequent grew his visits to the Untersberg, from each of which he returned with a thousand florins in gold, but with one less hair from his head; and for all that, he seemed not to be happy, for he saw only too clearly that he had

 The comet-drivers

bought only the appearance of love, and that his wife loved not him but only his money; and whenever he did not at once comply with her unreasonable and extravagant demands, she would treat him with contempt, so as to render life a burden to him. All this caused him a great deal of grief, which he sought to drown in the wine-cup. Thus he became at last a confirmed drunkard and an object of disgust. All the evil germs in his nature began to grow luxuriantly and to bear fruit. He became a weakling, a cruel tyrant towards his subjects, an abject coward in the presence of his wife, who treated him as if he were a slave. His troubles caused him to grow prematurely old, and the hair upon his head grew thinner from day to day.

Thus a few years passed away in great misery, and at last poor Burkhart was entirely bald-headed. The last florin was gone; but the countess had ordered a great tournament and dinner, to which many noblemen and ladies of rank were invited. Once more Burkhart went to the Untersberg for the purpose of asking the king of the gnomes for money; but no more hair did he have to give in return. The gnome appeared, and the knight, removing his helmet, showed him the deplorable condition of his scalp, hoping to arouse the pity of the king.

"Ah, Burkhart!" exclaimed Pypo; "did I not tell you to beware that your hairs may not become too few?"

"I now see my folly," sighed the knight; "but for pity's sake let me have only one more bag of gold, to save myself from disgrace."

"Ha! ha!" laughed the gnome. "Nothing brings nothing. No hair, no money; our bargain is at a end!"

"Ask what you will!" cried the knight; "but hair I have no more to give. Take my soul; but give me only one bag of money. Only one bag of gold I am asking of you!"

But in vain Burkhart implored the gnome. Pypo was inexorable, and laughed at him. This exasperated Burkhart, and becoming enraged, he cried: "Hell-hound! you have completed your devilish work. With each hair that you took from my head you robbed me of a part of my manhood. Now I recognise you as the fiend that you are. Give me back my lost energy. Give me back the beautiful golden hair of which you have despoiled me by means of your accursed gold. Give it back to me, or look out for the revenge of the Tollensteins!"

But the gnome laughed. "Fool!" he said; "do you wish to frighten me? Would you now curse the one from whom you received all that you wanted? I laugh at you and your threats; but if you wish your hair returned, be it so!"

So saying the gnome drew forth a cord twisted from Burkhart's hair, and threw it at the feet of the knight. He then disappeared within the depths of the Untersberg, while from all sides a mocking laughter shook the air, as if coming from a multitude of invisible spectators; but the knight went home and locked himself up in his bedroom.

At the castle of Tollenstein everything was in readiness for the beginning of the great tournament. Knights in glittering armour and ladies in costly dresses were thronging the halls; while in the courtyard below richly decked steeds, attended by grooms in bright colours, neighed and stamped the ground, impatient for the opening of the sham fight; for the beginning of which nothing was now needed but the presence of the host. The trumpets sounded, but nothing was seen of Burkhart. Repeatedly were messengers sent to his room, but they found the door locked and were not admitted. At last Julia, losing her patience, went up with clenched fists to inquire about the cause of this delay, but her knocks at the door elicited no reply. She therefore ordered the door to be forced open, and then a ghastly sight met her eyes. Burkhart von Tollenstein was lying dead on his bed, his features distorted as if he had died in great agony; around his neck was tied a cord of yellow human hair, with which he had been strangled; his eyes were protruding as if starting from their sockets; while his fingers were spasmodically closed around a bag containing one thousand florins in gold. This was the end of the Tollensteins.

And now the excuses for writing the following tale:

If this story of Burkhart of Tollenstein had never been exhumed from the archives containing the family histories of the ancient knights of the Duchy of Salzburg, the following chapters would never have been written; for it was the discovery of these reliable documents which recalled to my memory the history told to me by my now deceased friend, Mr Schneider, who was himself a participant in the adventure which I am about to describe.

It appears that, long after the death of Burkhart von Tollenstein, three very learned gentlemen, having heard of that story, arrived from some far-off country—presumably from the dark continent. Being of a very sceptical turn of mind, they did not believe in gnomes, and had undertaken their journey for the purpose of disproving the existence of the spirits of Nature. They belonged to a scientific Society, whose object was the abolition of the supernatural, and to sober up mankind by drawing away their attention from all sorts of ideals, and bring them back to the dry and hard facts of material life. That Society had already accomplished a great deal of important work. They had by a certain system of logic disproved the existence of God, spirit and soul, and shown that all that is called life or consciousness is nothing else but the result of friction brought on by the mechanical motion of molecules of dead matter accidentally coming into contact with each other. The three gentlemen with whom we shall directly become acquainted were appointed by the Society for the Abolition of the Supernatural as a committee, for the purpose of giving the last death-blow to the superstitious belief in spirits and gnomes, and arrived for that purpose. They were firmly determined that the belief in anything that could not be seen by means of corporeal eyes, or grasped with fingers of flesh, should be relegated into the garret, where antiquated superstitions are stowed away.

After due consultation, these gentlemen resolved to make a scientific expedition to one of the caves of the Untersberg, reported to be haunted; and Mr Schneider, being then a young and vigorous man, well acquainted with the topography of the mountain, was invited to accompany them. The excursion took place on the day preceding St John's, it being the 23rd of June; but the date of the year escaped my memory. The adventures which Mr Schneider experienced are told by him in the following pages.

II
IN THE DRAGON'S DEN

The Cave

ABOUT a thousand feet below the summit of the Untersberg, and not very far from the top of one of its spurs, that reaches out into the valley through which runs the limpid stream coming from the renowned lake called the "Koenigsee," there is a spacious cave, within an almost perpendicular slope of rocks, several hundred feet in height. This cave or hole, called the "Dragon's Den," is large enough for affording shelter to a whole herd of cattle, and high enough so that a good-sized church, steeple and all, might be put therein. Its roof is formed by an overhanging rock (as is shown in our picture), and the hole extends like a tunnel from one side of the hill to the other; so that if seen from below it appears like an archway through which the sky and the stars on the other side may be seen.

This den is said to have been inhabited in ancient times by a villainous dragon of a very peculiar kind, having no conscience, reason, or common sense, but being exceedingly selfish. His greatest pleasure was to dissect and analyse everything, and to destroy all that was of an ideal nature; to tear the clothes away from everything exalted and beautiful for the purpose of exposing bare facts. These he liked so well, that he imagined the bones of every creature were its only essential

The Dragon's Den

parts; so he tore the flesh of his victims away and devoured their bones. From the altitude of his den he would overlook both sides of the hill, and whenever he saw a pretty maiden wandering among the rocks in search of the Alpine rose or the Edelweiss, he would pounce upon her, drag her to his den, dissect her, and strip her of all flesh, and devour the bones piece by piece. It is said that later on the dragon emigrated

The comet-drivers

into the valley, but his den was selected by the committee for the investigation concerning the non-existence of gnomes.

Before we proceed further, it will be necessary to introduce the reader to our friends. There was, first of all, Professor Thomas Cracker, a member of nearly all scientific societies in the world, a great sceptic, who, by a long course of scientifically training his imagination, had acquired such a degree of scientific scepticism that he always knew everything without taking the trouble of looking at it. There was no fact in Nature for which he had not invented a theory; and if the theory did not fit it, so much the worse for the facts. He had become celebrated; because, owing to his superior sagacity, and after years of persevering study, he had succeeded in discovering that a certain book entitled "Little Alice in Wonderland," was only a fable, not based upon historical facts, and whose object was to bamboozle the ignorant and take in unwary and gullible people. Owing to the great merit obtained by this work the honour and title of a member of the Academy was bestowed upon him.

Mr Cracker's father had been the keeper of a variety shop, and was in the habit of ignoring and treating with contempt everything that was not of his own manufacture or kept in his shop. Nevertheless, among the good articles which he kept for sale, there were many things that had gone out of fashion. These he used to fit up in a new style, varnish and paint them over, give them new labels with modern names, and advertise them as something brand new. Thus he did a good trade and gained a reputation.

Professor Cracker, junior, resembled his father to a dot, only he traded in less tangible goods. He also was in the habit of ignoring and treating with contempt everything that did not agree with the theories that were manufactured by himself or his colleagues; nevertheless there were among his articles of creed certain doctrines taught centuries ago, but having gone out of fashion. These he used to take down from the garret where they had been forgotten, dress them up in modern style, varnish them over with modern expressions, label them with newly invented names, and advertise them as brand-new discoveries, or goods of his own invention. In this way Professor Cracker traded in science and gained a reputation.

The next was the Reverend Jeremiah Stiffbone, a clergyman, who had received from his congregation a liberal amount of money to enable him to travel in search of the truth that could not be found at home. Mr Stiffbone was well versed in all sorts of authorities, and able to quote almost any number of books in support of almost any opinion, for he knew the contents of many scientific and religious writings,—that is to say, he knew what was written therein; but as to his knowledge in regard to the subjects themselves, it would be difficult to decide what it was; for he one day believed in this and the next day in another author's veracity, and the one into whom he put his faith was for the time being to him the only infallible one. Thus he stumbled along upon the path of wisdom, falling from one opinion into another like a person in a state of intoxication. It should not be supposed, however, that Jeremiah loved this state of uncertainty and wavering. What he wanted, above all, was to establish a scientific and religious system that could be fully depended on as being true and reliable, and containing articles and scientific doctrines which everyone would have to accept as true, and go to sleep quietly, being firmly convinced that the opinions therein were the final dictates of science, incontrovertible, not subject to improvement, and fully correct.

As to the external appearance of the above-named two gentlemen, Professor Cracker was of short stature, thickly set, with a rubicund face, smoothly shaven, except a pair of grey side-whiskers. His little eyes continually wandered restlessly from one object to another, his arms were unusually long, but his legs short and bow-shaped, and all this somehow contributed to give him the appearance of a Mandril (Cynocephalus Maimon), as may be said without giving offence to the Professor; for he was himself firmly of the opinion that the whole of man had descended from the ape. He even looked with satisfaction upon his long line of ancestors, and prided himself on having become somehow superior to them in the art of reasoning, if not in bodily strength.

As to the Reverend Stiffbone, he seemed the reverse of Professor Cracker. He was thin and tall, looking like a collection of bones of some antediluvian bird. His features were sharp, his head almost bald, and his mouth wide, while his chin and nose were long and protruding, as if they were trying to meet each other. Upon his nose he wore a pair of green goggles of great size, causing him to appear not unlike an owl; but his nose and chin gave him a resemblance to one of the well-known wooden nut-crackers, which are manufactured in the city of Nuremberg, and are the delight of the children all over the world.

Finally, there was Moses Abraham Scalawag, Esq., the commercial business manager of the expedition. His external appearance went to show that he was not much of an idealist, but preferred the good and material things of this life, and had no aversion to a certain kind in spirits. Although he denounced the belief in hobgoblins, ghosts, gnomes, etc., as a degraded superstition, he somehow thought that, if the story of Burkhart von Tollenstein were true, it might be worth the while to investigate the financial condition of the gnomes in the Untersberg.

We were accompanied by a guide, carrying our provisions and scientific instruments. This guide was a direct descendant of the reputed Lazarus Gitschner, who in the year 1529 spent ten days among the gnomes in the Untersberg. We attempted to draw him out, but the guide would not reveal what his ancestor had seen during that visit; nor is this surprising, for Lazarus himself never revealed it to anybody except to the priest in the confessional. All that has become known about it is, that he came out of the Untersberg a man entirely changed from what he was before he went in, and the priest also, after hearing the confession, became very much changed himself, even so that he left off playing ninepins on Sunday morning, led a retired life, and died not long afterwards in the odour of sanctity.

Bright was the day, and the earth looked refreshed from the morning dew that still rested upon the daffodils and ferns, where it glittered in the light of the sun like so many small diamonds. The air was fragrant from the odour of pines and wild thyme, and the breeze carried up from the valley an aroma of new-mown hay. Peacefully grazed the goats upon the sides of a hill, from which rushed a small cataract in a thousand cascades, while an air of tranquillity and solemnity rested upon the scene below, interrupted only by the tolling of the bell in the distant village church, which sounded harmoniously into the solitude.

Of all this, however, our members of the committee saw, heard, smelt, and knew nothing; for each was absorbed in his own thoughts. Professor Cracker moved slowly on, carrying his wig on his walking-stick over his shoulder, and revelling in the anticipation of the glory which the annihilation of the gnome theory would bring upon him. The Rev. Stiffbone's long coat-tails fluttered in the wind as he marched on, taking long strides upon the uneven path, and his thoughts were absorbed in the prospect of being able to add another incontrovertible doctrine in regard to the non-existing of gnomes to his Bible of Science. Mr Scalawag wobbled along as well as he could, thinking nothing particular, but stopping frequently and wiping the sweat from his brow. At last he exclaimed:

"Confound these gnomes! Is it worth the while to climb

up to that den and waste our valuable time in disproving that such animals exist?"

To this the Reverend Stiffbone replied:

"Gnomes are not animals, but imaginary beings. Theophrastus Paracelsus describes them as being intellectual forces in nature, whatever that may mean. They are about six inches in height, but able to change and to elongate their bodies."

"But how can you determine their height," asked Mr Scalawag, "if they are merely imaginary? You may just as well imagine them to be a thousand feet, if you try."

"Rot!" interrupted Professor Cracker; for that was his favourite impression whenever anything was mentioned that was unknown to him. "Rot! there are no such things as intelligent forces of nature, neither imaginary ones nor others. This degrading superstition has now lasted long enough, and this day will make an end to such vagaries."

"Are you then firmly convinced," asked Mr Scalawag, rather dejectedly, "that the treasures of the gnomes in the Untersberg do not exist?"

"They exist only in the imagination of fools," replied the Professor. "There can be no such thing as a spirit, as I shall demonstrate to you to-day by means of my new spiritoscope."

"It is strange," now remarked the Rev. Stiffbone, "that there are still some respectable authorities favouring such a superstitious belief. Even the Bible mentions the existence of spirits in more than one instance."

"Rot!" replied the Professor. "There is no theory so absurd that it may not find admirers among otherwise intelligent people. Only think of the many fools who imagine it to be possible to make cars that are pulled by steam!"

"Do you then believe it to be absolutely impossible to make railways?" asked Mr Scalawag.

"Railways!" sneeringly exclaimed Cracker. "Rot! No man in his sane senses would ever think of such a thing. Steam can blow; but it cannot pull cars; if a steam-engine were invented, it would scald everybody to death. As to those eccentric and fanatical people who now fancy it possible to make a railway between Manchester and Liverpool, I have only to say that we, the scientists of this century, decline to waste our time in examining such wild and extravagant schemes. Even if the tales told in some of the newspapers were true, instead of being deplorable vagaries, and if it were possible to invent such an engine, it would not interest us, for surely nobody would be insane enough to trust his life and his safety to an engine going at the terrible speed of sixteen miles an hour! No, my dear sir! To make a railway is as impossible as that stones should fall from heaven; the reason of which impossibility the Academy of Science has pointed out, namely, because there are no stones in the sky."

It may be observed that this conversation took place before the time when meteors were known and railways in action; at the present time such a display of scientific ignorance would of course be impossible.

"Suppose," said the Rev. Stiffbone, "we admit for argument's sake that a railway could be made on a level plain. What would they do if they were to come to a mountain? They would have to dig a hole through it, pass through it in the dark, and coming out at the other end the passengers would suddenly emerge into the light. This sudden change would undoubtedly strike them blind."

"Undoubtedly it would," added Professor Cracker, "unless they were to wear travelling-goggles for protection. You may however rest assured that, if railways could be made, we would have discovered it long ago, and the same may be said in regard to gnomes, ghosts, spirits, or intelligent forces of any kind. If there were such things we would know it."

"How is it then possible," I asked, "that the ancient philosophers believed such things?"

"To a layman like you," answered the Professor, "such a question may be pardoned. The ancient philosophers were fools; they did not know as much as one of our schoolboys knows to-day. As to Lord Lytton, Goethe, and other more modern writers who spoke of such things, they only did so because they loved to make jokes for the amusement of the wise, and to have some fun at the expense of the gullible. We know that spirit without matter does not exist. Matter is visible; consequently the spirits would have to possess visible forms. We also know that no kind of living beings can exist within solid rocks, where they would be without water and air, and finally, if there were any intelligent forces in nature, they would know the importance of coming forward and proving their existence to men of science."

I remarked that a belief in gnomes was quite common in this country, and asked whether this could be explained.

"Ridiculously easy!" said the Professor. "The sources of error are—inherited idiosyncrasies; a want of scientific training in making observations; subjective, objective, and epidemic hallucinations; credulity, hysteria, suggestion, dreams, hypnotism, post-hypnotic auto-suggestion, and so forth."

"Nevertheless," I objected, "there are those who have been touched by gnomes, have seen and conversed with them, received tangible objects from them."

"Rot!" replied Cracker. "It is all due to wilful deception, humbug, swindle, trumpery, fraud, plagiarism, coincidence, telepathic impact, thought-transfer, unconscious cerebration, mediumship, sympathetic association of ideas, etc. Only recently I have discovered, after making a long research and consulting many authorities, that the accounts given in Gulliver's Travels were not based upon historical facts, but are only the products of the imagination of the author, who for thus imposing upon the credulity of the public, must be regarded as being one of the greatest cheats of his age. Fetch me a spirit or gnome, and let me dissect it to see of what it is made. Unless you do so, I say that it is nothing but rot, the product of the disordered fancy of a scientifically untrained brain."

I did not quite agree with Cracker's views, and I therefore said: "I believe that there are still people capable of telling a pigtail from a broomstick without dissecting it and having it certified to by a professor of science."

Cracker and Stiffbone exchanged an ominous look.

"This," said Stiffbone, "comes from the increased disrespect for the authorities. Nowadays everybody imagines that he has a right to think and say what he pleases. It is time that a law ought to be made punishing heresy in science, as it used to be punished in regard to religion. Not long ago I heard a new heresy preached about what they call 'conservation of energy.' Men ought not to be permitted to go about and poison the minds of the public by spreading erroneous scientific doctrines. We absolutely need a Bible of Science, stating exactly what scientific beliefs the people are to accept."

"Such a book," answered the Professor, "would be of the greatest benefit to the world, and prevent the injurious and misleading self-thinking done by laymen and ignorant tramps. What business have the common people to do their own thinking? No one ever attempts to make his own shoes or clothes, but leaves this to his shoemaker or tailor, who can do it much better, cheaper and quicker than he could do it himself. Why not apply the same system to deciding scientific or religious questions? Let the thinking in regard to such things be left to those who are trained and entitled to it."

With these views the Rev. Stiffbone fully agreed. "Science," he said, "ought to be left to the scientists, religion to the clergy, morality to the police, medicine to the physicians, money matters to bankers, and ideal things to legally appointed idealists. This would enable the people to give more attention to their own material interests. Instead of thinking about things which bring them no profit, they might employ their time for useful things, such as the raising of hogs. Religion ought not to be neglected, for the fear of the devil is the security of the Church; but one authentic sermon printed and posted every Sunday in public places would save the employment of an army of preachers, and moreover secure conformity to the doctrines taught everywhere. If the people must have music, one or two organ-grinders would be enough for a town of no more than a thousand inhabitants; if they wanted poetry, one well-trained and diplomatised verse-maker could supply the whole country."

"These questions," said M. Scalawag, Esq., "deserve the most careful consideration. Time is money. The struggle for existence is the first law among all beings; the survival of the fittest its necessary result. Let everyone take as much care as he can of his own interest, and leave it to those who are appointed for that purpose to look out for the rest."

"We are appointed for that," exclaimed Professor Cracker, "and we will attend to it. I have just discovered a new system of hypnotism by means of which large crowds can be hypnotised at once. Instead of sending the children to school, we will hypnotise into their heads all that we want them to know, and cause them to post-hypnotically forget all which we do not wish them to remember. Thus we will be the kings of the world, and all mankind will dance as we pull the strings!"

While carrying on these discussions we arrived at the "Dragon's Den," where our investigations were to begin. The place showed no indication of the presence of spirit; there was nothing dismal about it; on the contrary, an air of peace seemed to rest upon the scene. At the entrance of the cave there was a wild rosebush of considerable size and some Alpine flowers, among which I noticed the Larkspur and Belladonna. The walls consisted of marble rocks, exhibiting a variety of colours, and were covered in some places with mosses and ferns. In a shady corner there was still a remnant of snow, resembling a miniature glacier, and rendering the air cool and pleasant. The two openings at the sides offered a magnificent view.

The guide—who had remained a little behind, as his movements were greatly impeded by the legs of Professor Cracker's spiritoscope, which he carried—now arrived with his bag of provisions, and unpacked his treasures. Cold meats, poultry and cheese, ham and eggs, butter and bread, made their appearance, and were soon disposed of by the committee. Beer and wine had not been forgotten, and Professor Cracker, filling his glass with champagne, lifted it up and offered a toast, "to the annihilation of the gnomes;" which was followed by another toast, pronounced by Jeremiah Stiffbone, "to Professor Cracker, the king of science, and inventor of the spiritoscope," while Mr Scalawag, in offering his sentiments, said he hoped to find some of the treasures of the Untersberg.

After the refreshments were taken, the investigations began. To begin with, the committee carefully examined the rocks and walls and every nook and corner of the "Dragon's Den" for the purpose of convincing themselves that there was no place where anybody might hide himself and play a practical joke upon the investigators. They measured the size of the rocks, and made sure of their solidity and the entire absence of any subterranean caves or holes. The floor was found to be perfectly solid, and no gnomes were to be seen. Thereupon they carefully noted the hour and the minute, as is always necessary on such occasions, and evidence was taken that the sky was clear. The direction of the wind was determined with great accuracy, and found to be E.N.E.; the temperature was taken and the various thermometers

 The comet-drivers

indicated—25° Celsius, 20° Reaumur, and 77° Fahrenheit; the barometer showed an elevation of 5800 feet above the sea and a medium atmospheric pressure. No gnome or spirit of any kind appeared upon the scene, nor was there to be found anything whatever of a spiritual character. After all the necessary preparations were made Professor Cracker produced his spiritoscope, whose description we are permitted to give for the benefit of all psychical researchers; and as a boon to the whole of mankind:

Dr Cracker's Spiritoscope

This ingeniously constructed and very simple, although somewhat ponderous instrument was the original invention of Professor Cracker, and enabled him, instead of directly looking at an object, to behold and examine it by means of a series of reflections produced by four scientifically arranged

THE SCIENTIFIC INVESTIGATION

mirrors bent towards each other at angles of 45 degrees.

The main body of the instrument consisted of a wooden box in which the four above-named mirrors were placed so as to face each other, and to the box was attached a telescope-tube. Thus a ray of light coming from an outside object and entering the box would produce an image in the first mirror; this would become reflected in the second and third, and finally in the fourth, where it could be seen through the telescope.

The whole apparatus was mounted upon a tripod with movable legs, so that it could be turned in every direction.

It will naturally be asked, how could Professor Cracker expect by such natural meansto discover anything supernatural, and what is the benefit of looking at the reflection of a thing in a mirror, if it might be just as well seen directly with the eye? As to the first question, Professor Cracker did not admit the existence of anything beyond the common aspect of nature, and needed therefore no instrument for its discovery; while in regard to the second question, he said that direct vision was unscientific and unreliable, because what a man sees, or believes to see, may be caused by irregular cerebral action, hallucination, defective sight, ecstasy, trance, clairvoyance, or other diseases; but mirrors could not be deceived—they would not become hallucinated, or enter into a state of ecstasy:—they only showed what was actually true, and there was no humbug about them. Direct sight was well enough for common people with common sense, but indirect vision for science.

Heretofore the great merit of this spiritoscope was, as Professor Cracker repeatedly pointed out, that it had never produced any other than negative results, but these had been obtained unfailingly on all occasions, for it had actually never indicated the presence of any genius, gnome, ghost, or spirit whatever; but as the instrument was constructed according to unquestionable principles, these negative results were fully sufficient to prove the correctness of Professor Cracker's

The comet-drivers

theory.

On this occasion, however, there seemed to be something the matter with the spiritoscope. Be it that the mirrors were not in order, or that even scientific and indirect vision may be deceptive, there was evidently some kind of an obscuration within the tube, which could not be explained by natural causes. In vain Professor Cracker repeatedly cleaned his spectacles, and ultimately substituted coloured glasses for them; the fact was undeniable that something dark, some sort of a shadow, appeared repeatedly within the field of indirec vision, and this something must have been alive, for it moved about by means of some energy contained within itself, and without being kinetically impelled by any discoverable extraneous force. Repeatedly the Professor exclaimed the ominous word: "rot!" and "bosh!" and "impossible!" His scepticism had to give way before the evidence produced by his spiritoscope, and at last he was overcome by the conviction of having discovered a gnome. He looked somewhat pale, as with bated breath and with ill-suppressed excitement he announced the discovery to his colleagues.

It was now Rev. Stiffbone's turn to take a look through the spiritoscope. He, too, saw the shadow, and saw it move. Owing to the circumstance that the light fell into the instrument from the side opposed to the standpoint of the observer, the part of the spirit turned toward Stiffbone's eye could not be clearly seen, but its outlines seemed to grow sometimes larger and sometimes smaller, from which he inferred that the spirit was a gnome, as they were said to be able to change the size of their forms.

These observations were corroborated by Mr Scalawag. Professor Cracker looked again, and having satisfied himself that there could be no possible mistake, he made a speech, in which he said that it had been reserved for him to make the greatest discovery of this age, and that the existence of gnomes—which had heretofore been doubted by certain too sceptical people—was now an established fact, demonstrated by him for the first time in human history.

But alas! "this world is but a fleeting show," and even the demonstrations of science cannot always be depended upon as absolutely true, for while the Professor made his speech, the head of a little mouse appeared at the opening of the tube, and seeing the coast clear, the mouse jumped to the ground and ran away. How the mouse happened to come into the spiritoscope has never been satisfactorily explained. The committee looked perplexed, and Cracker grew red in the face.

"Errare humanum est!" exclaimed Stiffbone, and Mr Scalawag added: "We are all liars. The best plan will be to say nothing about it."

Although the committee did not believe thenceforth in spirits, it can nevertheless not be denied that a spirit of gloom rested upon them after this incident; a scowl rested upon the Professor's face, and he admitted that for once in his life he had been mistaken.

While they discussed this matter the wind had changed from E.N.E. to N., and now a light puff of air brought a piece of paper flying into the cave. Rev. Stiffbone saw it, and picked it up. There were written upon it the following verses:—

O foolish mortal, by dull senses bound;

Within thyself the spirit must be found.

Know thou thyself, and by self-knowledge know

The lives above and in the world below.

In every sphere each being knows its own;

To spirits only spirits can be shown.

After reading these lines, Mr Stiffbone handed the paper to the Professor, and asked him what he thought. The Professor carefully examined the structure of the paper and said:

"This is nothing but an ordinary piece of notepaper,

manufactured in this country. There is nothing supernatural about it."

"But the verses," answered Stiffbone. "They seem to refer to the subject of our conversation. How is this coincidence to be explained?"

"In a very simple manner," replied Professor Cracker, growing more and more excited as he spoke. "You, sir, have written these miserable verses yourself, for the purpose of playing it on me; but let me assure you that, even if I have been imposed on by a mouse, I am not going to be fooled by such a ragamuffin as yourself; your trick was not clever enough for that."

During this speech the Rev. Stiffbone, with open mouth, stared aghast at the Professor, and the word "ragamuffin" aroused his temper. He said that such an ill-founded accusation was calculated to greatly lessen his respect for one whose capacity to judge he had anyhow always regarded as doubtful, and that he owed it to his own respectability as a clergyman to regard Mr Cracker's calumnies as being those of a man in his dotage, if not a wilful perverter of truth.

Cracker retorted again, and it is doubtful how the matter would have ended, but just at that moment a long-drawn sigh was heard, coming from some invisible source, and at the next moment a gust of wind followed that overthrew the spiritoscope, and sent Stiffbone's hat flying out at the other end of the Dragon's Den. Directly afterwards the cave became illumined by a flash of lightning, and this was succeeded by a clap of thunder which caused the ground to tremble, and reverberated like the firing of a battery of guns through the clefts in the neighbourhood. The committee stood aghast and terrified, looking at each other in a perplexed manner and not knowing what to do.

It appears that the sky had become suddenly overcast with clouds, and a storm gathered at the top of the Untersberg, while our friends were too much absorbed in their scientific researches to notice it, and now the rain began to come down in torrents, and the archway offered but little protection, for sheets of rain were blown in at the open side of the cave, and streams of water began to flow in every direction over the ground.

In a few moments the members of the committee and myself were drenched to the skin, and did not know what to begin; but our guide, drawing aside the branches of the rosebush that stood at the entrance, pointed out to us an excavation in the rock, which had escaped the observation of the committee, and he invited us to enter. Into this hole we crawled one after another; and after proceeding a few feet it grew wider, and formed a hollow of considerable size. Here we were comfortable enough, only we were wet, and the place was perfectly dark.

Professor Cracker struck a light, and lit a candle which he happened to have in his pocket, and by that aid we discovered a passage leading still further into the interior of the hill. This we decided to explore. Professor Cracker entered with his candle, then came Rev. Stiffbone, after him Mr Scalawag, and finally myself, each man holding on to the coat-tail of the one who preceded.

Thus we went on for a considerable distance, when suddenly a draught of cold air blew out the Professor's light. At the same time Mr Cracker's foot hit against some soft elastic substance of an unknowable kind, and directly afterwards he received a fearful blow upon his abdomen from something unseen. Turning round for escaping the invisible enemy, he received another blow that sent him flying heels over head, overturning the Rev. Stiffbone, who in his turn upset Mr Scalawag. They were all lying in a heap, and I heard Cracker's voice producing a series of most unearthly yells; but the Rev. Stiffbone, while begging for mercy and blindly grasping about, clutched the

The comet-drivers

air and got hold of Mr Scalawag's hair, who defended himself with his fists; but my observations were also cut short, for I had just time, as my eyes became accustomed to the darkness, to see a still darker object rushing at me over the prostrate forms of my friends, when I myself received a severe blow upon my stomach, that caused me to lose my senses, and for a moment I knew nothing more.

III
WITHIN THE UNTERSBERG

THE GROTTO OF THE NYMPHS

IT seems that during the consternation caused by this event, I must have unconsciously wandered off, for when I gathered my senses again, I found myself in a strange labyrinth of rocks. In vain I tried to find my way back to the Dragon's Den; there were perpendicular walls and precipices encompassing me on all sides, and the only outlet which I discovered led me still higher up towards the main body of the Untersberg.

The storm-clouds had disappeared and the sky was clear; but my mind (if there is such a thing) was somewhat confused; I did not know which was which. Owing to Professor Cracker's exposition about the unreliability of direct vision, I could not tell whether the things around me were actually there, or whether they were merely the products of auto-suggestion, trumpery, etc. More than once I bumped my head against a projecting rock, because my method of observation was not scientifically trained enough to enable me to realise the actuality of the rock without a knock-down argument. I had always fancied before that if one receives an impression from

The comet-drivers

an object, be it in the waking state or in a dream, an object or image of some kind must be actually present, from which that impression comes; but now I saw that, according to science, impressions may come from nothing and may be only the products of the accidental friction of brain molecules. I was therefore no longer sure of the existence of anything that had not been analysed and attested to by a scientific expert.

It seemed to me that the sun was about to set, and that I was still wandering on, querying whether I actually was myself or whether some gnome was playing a trick upon my imagination, making me believe that I was I. There was nothing to prove to me scientifically that the something or nothing which imagined itself to be myself was not something else, entirely unknown to me, provided there was such a thing as "myself" at all, which seemed rather doubtful, it having not yet been analysed and its composition shown. I can, in truth, only say that something which somehow seemed to be myself (but to whom it seemed so, I do not know) imagined itself to be I; but, for all I know, there may be no "I," and it may have been nothing but space.

It seemed to me, or to something, that the setting sun was gilding the ice-fields of the neighbouring mountain-peaks with floods of light, and I (or something) received or seemed to receive the impression somehow, that tints of various hues, beginning with a dainty rose-colour, followed by orange, yellow, sea-green, and ending with blue, were adorning the sky (if there was any), while clouds, apparently floating within the depths of space (whose existence has not yet been proved scientifically), seemed to appear like fleecy masses of pure silver, lined with fluid gold. The vegetation (provided that there actually was one) appeared to be more scanty than below, and to consist mainly of clusters of Rhododendron, and occasionally a specimen of Mandrake, Gentian, or Thyme was to be seen or imagined. Judging from certain impressions, which something that seemed to be myself appeared to receive,

I seemed to arrive at the conclusion that there were rocks covered with green moss, upon which grew various ferns and some Ericas. Tranquillity somehow seemed to reign supreme in this altitude, although this is a mere assertion, which I am not prepared to prove; and I seemed to perceive nothing which could have led anyone to infer that the stillness was in any way interrupted, except by the song of a finch that was sitting or appeared to sit upon the branch of a tree—always supposing that the tree was actually there—and the croaking of a flock of ravens, which were flying or seemed to be flying around the tops of the Untersberg. I say all this with a certain reserve, and confess myself unable to prove it; because direct vision is unreliable, and I had no spiritoscope at my command.

I say that all this seemed (to whom?) to be as described; but even this is not scientifically exact or correct; for not knowing myself, how could I have the cheek to assert that I actually perceived anything, or nothing, or everything? How could I make any exact statement about myself if I am not acquainted with myself, and do not know whether or not I exist? I love to be scientifically exact in my statements, and to avoid making wild assertions. I wish (or imagine to wish) to express myself in a manner leaving no room for the learned critic to misunderstand or misinterpret my words, and to speak so plainly that everybody must necessarily understand what I mean; but I find that this philosophical and round-about way of describing things is very inconvenient, and that for the reader's own sake I cannot persevere in it. Everything in this world seems to be only relatively true, and if we were bound to speak nothing but absolute truth, and express it in a manner that could not possibly be misunderstood by anybody, we would surely be doomed to eternal silence. I must therefore ask the permission of the reader to depart from this exact and strictly scientific method of speaking and circumscribing, and to do like people of common sense, and tell what I experienced or believed to experience, as if I were really something whose existence had been proved and recognised by science, even if I have no other proof of my existence to offer, except that I am. This being myself is a reality to me, but it may be discredited by another; for there can be nothing real to anybody except what he or she realises, and if they realise it, it is, or seems to be, real to them. During my visit in the Untersberg I realised my existence, or seemed to realise it just as much as at any other time in my life (always provided that I exist and live), and the experiences through which I passed were just as real to me as any other experiences before or after that event. Let those who doubt my words, or deny the possibility of what I describe as having occurred, doubt or deny to their heart's content; they cannot rob me of the satisfaction of knowing what I know.

Somehow I felt myself more free than usual; my body moved without experiencing any fatigue, and I seemed to have no weight. Owing, perhaps, to the invigorating influence of the mountain air, I felt myself filled with strength; my mind was tranquil, my heart full of joy, and, as it were, one with the spirit of all nature—if I may be permitted to use such an expression—and it may be for this reason that I understood the language of nature as plainly as if it had been expressed in audible words, for the rushing of a distant waterfall spoke to me of eternal motion; the presence of the earth of the substantiality of the universe, nourishing all things; the wide expanse of the air of universal freedom; and the fiery orb of the sinking sun of an universal consciousness whose existence cannot be proved, but which may be experienced by souls that are free. Even the flowers had a language of their own, speaking to me of purity, beauty, modesty, and similar principles unknown to modern science, and not yet analysed and classified.

As I scrambled on the scenery grew more wild. Huge boulders of enormous size often blocked the way, throwing fantastic shadows upon the ground. Slowly the sun disappeared behind the slopes of the western range, and solitary stars began to glitter here and there in the sky. The song of the finch had ceased, and the ravens gone to roost among the tops of the pines; but the more all animated things became silent and quiet, the more seemed life to become active in those things which are called inanimate—it was as if the inner life of nature awakened while the outward life went to rest. There is a voice that speaks to the soul in the stillness of night with words that are not to be found in the dictionary. Of course, Professor Cracker would surely call this an hallucination or lie; but, for all that, I know it to be true. The boulders around me looked like gigantic sentinels guarding the entrance to the kingdom of the gnomes, and asking me in their own language by what right I dared to enter upon the forbidden precinct. Here and there the trunk of a stunted tree, a larch or fir with crooked boughs, added to the grotesqueness of the picture, complaining to me bitterly in silent but nevertheless eloquent words that the soil in that place was too poor and the climate too rough to permit a full development of its qualities and a luxuriant evolution of form. At last I stood before a wall of rocks, at the bottom of which a dark cavern held its jaws permanently open, and a feeling of curiosity attracted me towards the entrance. I felt a sort of premonition that the mysterious depths of that cavern was holding for me a new revelation.

The night had now fairly set in, but the moon arose in her glory. It was, as already stated, the eve of St John's Day, when fairies and elves are said to come nearer to our world to hold intercourse with mortals; the mysterious night, when the ruby spark in the heart of the fern may be seen. A feeling of awe came over me as I looked into the cave and saw the silvery rays of the rising moon shining through the opening, revealing within the interior a lake of considerable extent. I went nearer, and now I beheld, as far as I could see, perpendicular rocks bordering the lake, with projecting nooks, holes, and crevices

     The comet-drivers

of unknown extent, while, from the vaulted roofs, appearing like huge stalactites of curious shapes, a curtain of icicles descended, and the surface of the water glittered and sparkled in the moonlight, and the grotto looked like the cave of the nymphs in a fairy tale. I strained my eyes to behold the further end of the lake, but the background was veiled in darkness, and my sight could not penetrate through the mysterious gloom.

Something seemed to draw my soul towards the realm of that shadow which the rays of the moon could not reach, and, as I stood listening, a soft melody was wafted over the waters. Was it the breeze causing a rippling upon the surface which produced that melodious sound while playing among the icicles, or was it the rhythmic dripping of drops of water from the vault overhead, causing faint echoes within these secret recesses? I cannot tell, but it seemed to me like a tiny voice of a woman, but of a woman of some ethereal kind. The melody seemed to express a longing for something unknown. It was like the cry of a new-born soul, desiring to live and exist.

It seems to me an impossibility to fully express in words the sentiments that were embodied in that song. It contained a desire for death or transformation—terms which mean the same thing, namely, the abandoning one state of existence for another one. It embodied a wish for entering upon a higher plane of life and consciousness. The melody which I heard formed itself into a language, whose meaning may perhaps be approximately expressed in the following words:—

"O what is this secret longing,

Welling up within my heart?

Unknown powers, surging, thronging,

Rending solid rocks apart.

New-born joys and dying sadness,

Bursting clouds and opening sight!

Something whispers, full of gladness,

This is love, is life and light!"

These words formed themselves within myself without any conscious volition or ratiocination of my own; and, what is still more surprising, they had a certain magical effect upon me. I felt as if I were myself entering into a new state of consciousness, such as I never experienced before or afterwards, and as if I had become a new being, endowed with a new kind of perception and memory; it was as if I had been asleep all my life and suddenly awakened for the first time. I now somehow knew that I was I; but I could dissect or analyse my Self. I knew that my Self was a unity and not a compound, and therefore incapable of being taken to pieces. I had never known it before, and knew of no authority on whose strength I would have accepted that theory; nevertheless I was certain of it; because I found that my self-consciousness was not composed of parts.

And lo! as I stood at the border of that lake, bending forwards, and with all my senses on the alert listening to the song, I saw a radiance within the depths of that darkness, issuing from a circular luminous centre; and as I concentrated all my attention upon it, this light grew brighter, and there appeared in it the shape of a human being—a woman of supernatural beauty, in a mist-like, silvery garment dotted with stars. Her long golden hair was flowing over her shoulders, and a radiant light shone upon her forehead. It was that light, issuing, as I found afterwards, from a precious gem, which illuminated her person and all the objects within its sphere.

I dislike to tell what followed, because I have no means of demonstrating its truth, and there will be undoubtedly many inclined to doubt it or to dispute it away; but if I had to give evidence before a notary-public, I could not describe what followed otherwise than by saying that I was filled with an irresistible desire to approach that ethereal being, and that I

The comet-drivers

made a step forward, quite without being aware that I was stepping upon a lake. To my surprise, the water supported me, and I now think that it must have been solid ice, for I passed safely over it, and a moment afterwards I stood in mute admiration before the most charming apparition of a lady of noble mien. The lady of the lake looked at me with wondering eyes and smiled. This encouraged me, so I said:

"Who are you, angelic being? if you will permit an intruder this question. Are you one of the angels of heaven or a spirit of nature?"

"My name is Adalga," answered the lady, and her voice sounded like the music of the spheres. "I am the daughter of Bimbam I., King of the gnomes. But what are you? Are you a spirit, hobgoblin, or spook?"

"I am neither the one nor the other," I answered. "I am——" but at this moment I could not for the sake of my life remember who or what I was; I had entirely forgotten my name and all that referred to my past life. At last, while I was trying hard to remember who I was, it suddenly dawned upon me that I was an Irishman, born near the Lakes of Killarney, and living at Limerick. I am sure that if I ever was an Irishman, it must have been before I was born; but at that moment I was quite certain of it, and remembered my home and my family. I therefore said:—

"I am Patrick Mulligan, Esq., if it pleases your worship."

"There is a great deal of power in that name," replied the princess; "but what is your essential nature?"

"A tailor, if you please," was my answer; but seeing that the lady did not understand what I meant, I explained that I was in the habit of making clothes. Upon this she asked:

"Are you, then, one of these semi-intelligent forces of nature, capable of assuming a form, which according to our traditions are believed to inhabit the solid vastness of the element called the air?—one of these airy elementals whose bodies are subject to change—mischievous beings, that often cause explosions in our mines?"

The princess stared at me and I stared at her. What she said about the solid vastnesses of the air was incomprehensible to me, until I found out later on that the element of the air is just as impenetrable to the gnomes as the earth is to us; but what astonished me most was, that after having doubted the existence of elemental spirits of nature, I now found myself by one of them regarded as an elemental spirit of the air. At last I said: "With your permission, I flatter myself to be somewhat more than semi-intelligent, and if I am a force, I am surely a substantial one. The fact is that I am a man, a member of the human family, a gentleman from the ancient kingdom of Ireland and a descendant of Caolbha, the 123rd king of Ulster."

"A man! a gentleman!" exclaimed the princess, full of astonishment and surprise—as if it was the most unheard-of thing that one should be a man; and as if men and gentlemen were not much more plentiful in our world than gnomes and ghosts. This rather amused me, and I said to the princess:

"I hope that I did not give offence to your honour. It seems that you are leading a very retired life, as you have never seen a man."

But the princess paid little attention to what I said. Looking at me with her eyes wide open, she repeated, as if trying to persuade herself: "A man!"

"Of course a man," said I. "What else could I be?"

"I have been told of the existence of such superior beings," at last said the princess. "Our sages teach that they belonged to a now extinct race of divine or semi-divine beings, who were kings of creation, and to whom all the laws of nature were subservient. They were said to be gods, and even superior to the gods in wisdom and power; and that they were spirits, who sometimes assumed material bodies for the purpose of

                    The comet-drivers

studying the conditions of the lower kingdom of matter."

My vanity became excited by the description which the princess made of aboriginal man, and I did not wish to depreciate the good opinion which she had formed of me; so I merely nodded consent.

"And from what region of the wide empyrean have you descended?" continued the princess, folding her hands, as if filled with admiration and reverence.

"It is from Limerick that I come," was my answer.

"I have never heard of that region of space," said the princess, "nor did I ever see any of the immortal beings who inhabit that sphere; but it is sufficient for me to know that you are a man, and that I am permitted to worship you. My love to you is unbounded; all that I am belongs to you; to become united with you for ever is my only desire. Let me adore you. In you I shall find eternal life!"

No words can express the looks of love and affection which the princess bestowed upon me while her rosy lips expressed these sentiments, and she sank down before me in an attitude of worship. I at once thought that there must be a mistake somewhere, and that she took me for something higher than I knew myself to be; but I did not wish to disappoint her. The straightforwardness of the princess in speaking out her sentiments in plain language and without any mock modesty delighted me very much. I then did not know that this was originally a natural quality of the gnomes, who, being themselves born out of emotions, cannot disguise the emotions which cause them to live. So I replied:

"I highly appreciate your condescension, madame. I do not doubt the sincerity of your words; and as I am fortunately not a married man, there is no objection to our entering into very friendly and intimate relations with each other."

I do not know whether or not the princess understood what I said; but she continued to indulge in her expressions of love and admiration. Bending low, and extending her beautiful white arms towards me, she cried out in rapture—

"Let me worship thee, O self-born, self-existent one, thee who was before the world came into existence, and who will remain what he is even if all things perish! Thou, who knowest no death, let me embrace thee, and become one with thy divine nature! Let me hail thee, O son of wisdom and lord of creation, whose kingdom encompasses the sky, the earth, and the whole universe, whose Self includes and penetrates all, to whom all power belongs and all glory is due. O infinite one, having shown thyself to me in a limited form, let me dissolve in the infinitude of thy being. Tell me, O man, how I may serve thee!"

I was very much puzzled by this speech, and somehow felt that I did not deserve it. I had never known myself to be such a superior being as the princess described; but I saw that she was happy in her delusion, which afforded me a good opportunity to get my wish fulfilled, and obtain some knowledge in regard to the life of the gnomes. There was now a good chance to get the better of Professor Cracker and the likes of him. I therefore said:

"It is I, madame, who would always be at your service; but if you would do me a favour, I would, with your permission, take a look into the kingdom of the gnomes."

Thereupon the princess crossed her hands upon her bosom and bowing low, she said:

"Thy wish, O beloved and all-knowing one, is to me a command. Nothing shall hereafter separate me from thy glorious presence. Follow me, O my lord!"

Having spoken these words, her form dissolved, losing its human shape, and becoming, as it were, a ball of light with a fiery centre. This ball floated away and I followed. Was it that there was something the matter with the rocks or with myself? The walls of rock offered no resistance; we passed through them as we would pass through a London fog. It was such a strange experience that, if I did not know myself, I should be inclined to doubt my own words.

We might have been travelling for about ten minutes at the rate of what I should judge to have been about ten miles an hour, the princess literally acting as my guiding star, when the fog seemed to retreat on both sides, and in the open space I saw at a short distance a lot of other luminous balls, and in the midst of each there was a human-like form with a star upon the forehead, from which issued the light that formed the luminous spheres in which these beings lived and moved, each having its own peculiar light. Directly we entered, and were in the midst of the gnomes. They were of various sizes and colours. Some were nearly as tall as I, others like dwarfs. They were not all of the same brightness; some were more luminous than others and their stars more radiant. They had all some sort of an occupation. Some were quarrying marble, from which they made works of art and curious implements; others were engaged in mining. By some means, which I afterwards found to be the application of a substantial energy, which might be called liquid electricity, they rendered fluid the gold that glittered in yellow veins within the snow-white quartz, and after letting it run into moulds the gold became again solid and hard. There was no other light than what emanated from the gnomes themselves, and I saw that the amount of light in each individual indicated the amount of his or her spiritual energy and intelligence. Those that were luminous seemed to be very clever; others, emitting only a faint glow, looked dull and stupid, and between these two extremes there were luminous spheres and radiating stars of different degrees of brightness, exhibiting various tints and hues; but in the majority of them a tint of green could be perceived. They were what may be called "spirits," in spite of all that may be said to the contrary by Professor Cracker, and their bodies were of a substantial kind. Their forms were not permanent, nor were they, as spirits, dependent upon the existence of their forms. In their normal and spiritual condition they were like individual currents of air, that blow here and there, having no particular shape; but they assumed or projected corporeal and organised bodies whenever it was necessary for them to do so for the purpose of accomplishing some labour requiring a form; and in such cases each spirit assumed the same form again which he had before he dissolved, and which corresponded to his individual character; and he did this, not as a matter of choice, but of necessity, for such is the law of their nature, that to each character belongs a certain form of expression. A good gnome always assumes the same beautiful shape which he had in his previous embodiment, and whenever a wicked gnome dissolved and again took form, he acquired again the same distorted shape, the same features and clothing as before.

But this is a digression, and I must continue my account.

At my approach those who beheld me first were very much frightened, and dissolved into spheres of light, which grew less luminous as they expanded. This called the attention of the rest to my presence, whereupon what I would call a general scattering and dissolving took place; everybody vanished, and from all sides resounded the cries: "A spook! a hobgoblin! a ghost!"

Even the princess became affected by the general panic, so that she lost her presence of mind and disappeared, and the place would have been completely dark but for the fact that in the place of each gnome there was a fiery spark, corresponding in colour to the light that belonged to each individual. Thus the whole place was dotted with sparks of various colours, resembling jewels emitting magnetic rays. In the place of Adalga there was a beautiful pearl; there were brilliant diamonds, sapphires emitting a fine blue light, red-glowing rubies, glittering emeralds, amethysts, smaragds, and other jewels of various kinds—some very tiny, others of

   The comet-drivers

considerable size, but all had the same mysterious lustre, the same quality of fire; the difference was only in the amount and colour of the light they emitted.

I then remembered some tale which I had heard of people who went into the Untersberg and found untold treasures of gold and silver and precious stones, but were too much dazzled by the sight of so much wealth that they entirely forgot to pocket any of the jewels, and thought of it only after returning with empty hands. I therefore made up my mind not to lose this opportunity, and started to take one precious emerald, but a faint, childlike voice cried out to me:—

"Touch me not! touch me not!"

I then stretched out my hand towards others; but from each and every one came the same answer—"Touch me not!" However, I was not to be disappointed; so I gathered my courage and made a resolute grab at a great diamond; but on doing so I received an electric shock that threw me upon the ground. At the same time a clap of thunder reverberated through the hall, and the next moment the precious stones had disappeared, and I stood in the midst of a crowd of gnomes, who were talking and gesticulating in an excited manner. They all looked upon me with indignation, and even Adalga's face expressed disappointment and doubt. But one of the gnomes, a very bright fellow, the one who had been the diamond, came forward, and, assuming a threatening attitude, shook his fist at me and angrily exclaimed—

"This spectre has attempted my life. Why should we be afraid of a ghost that has no substance and is merely a compound of delusions? Let us drive it away! Make it vanish!"

In answer to this, and as if by common consent, all the gnomes shook their fists and cried—

"Put it out! let it be evaporated!"

"This is a queer reception," I said to the princess. "It is quite unexpected. I am neither a spectre nor a ghost, and not prepared to evaporate. I am a man!"

Then the princess came forward, and holding up her hand as a sign that everyone should be silent, she said—

"Do him no harm. Touch him not. He is a man!"

"A man!" exclaimed the gnomes, pushing forward and staring at me, while the one who had spoken first asked the princess—

"How do you perceive him to be a man?"

"He told me so himself!" answered the princess.

A general "Ah!" was the reply of the gnomes. "He said so himself! He told it to her!" they whispered to each other. The threatening attitude of the gnomes at once changed into one of respect. "A man!" they exclaimed, and the cry was repeated until from all parts of the open space it was echoed back by many voices shouting, "A man!" And through all the caves of the Untersberg the cry was resounded, "A man has come among us! A man! Let his name be blessed! All hail to Mulligan, the saviour of our world!"

Now from all sides gnomes came forward and stared at me. Some were old and others were young, men, women, and children, some dressed in jackets, others in gowns, many wearing hoods upon their heads, whose pointed ends hung down over their backs. I could not quite understand why they should be so much surprised at seeing a man, and expressed my surprise about it, saying that in the world where I lived men were as plentiful as bugs on a tree, while gnomes were exceedingly scarce, so that hardly anybody seriously believed in their existence, and that nobody would dare to say openly that he ever saw a gnome, for fear that somebody might laugh in his face.

Much better would it have been for me if I had been less loquacious, for I saw that some of the more intelligent gnomes looked now very indignant, and one of the wise ones came forward and said—

"Although you said yourself that you were a man, nevertheless I perceive in you only an inferior being, perhaps a hobgoblin; for how is it possible that men, being omnipotent and all-knowing spirits, should not know that we exist, and that they would be afraid of speaking the truth? Only a blaspheming elemental would dare to say that real men were subject to animal passions. How could the creator of all be ignorant of the existence of his creatures? How could he who rests on his own self-consciousness, and is affected by nothing, suffer from fear?"

I did not know what to say; but while trying to think of an answer to subdue the rising storm, for I saw that the gnomes were getting angry, the attention of the crowd was attracted towards the further end of the hall, where a large globe of yellow light appeared, which in coming nearer became condensed into a human form, appearing as a gnome of venerable aspect, with a jewel looking like a fiery topaz upon his head. He had a white beard, and was dressed in a black cloak or cape, and short trousers, stockings, and buckled shoes. In his hand he held something that looked like a tube or telescope. He was, as I heard them say, Prince Cravatu, minister to the king.

As he approached, all the gnomes became silent and waited in mute expectation for what he would have to say. He came up to me very close, and looked at me through his tube, which turned out to be a spiritoscope. The time during which he examined me seemed to me an eternity, but at last he finished, and spoke the ominous words—"Umbra simiæ vulgaris."

I knew enough Latin to understand that he said I was the ghost of a common ape. A general laughter arose, which was followed by murmurs of dissatisfaction. Cravatu's unkind remark wounded my feelings, and I therefore said—

"It is perhaps yourself who is a ghost and a monkey,

Mr Smarty! I am a man, and never had any monkey in my family. My father was Thomas Mulligan, a member of as good standing in the Church as anybody, and my mother's name was Bridget O'Flannigan, and they were married by Father Murphy, the parish priest." And talking myself into a sort of excitement, I proceeded to pull off my coat, and continued: "Just come out of here, you brute, and I will show you whether or not I am a man. I will blacken your eyes and turn you into a kettle-drum. I will make you think that a thousand monkeys have come to scratch your head, you blackguard!"

It was evident that among all present there was none who understood my speech, and Adalga seemed to listen to it with delight. Cravatu looked again and said, addressing the gnomes—

"He is from the land of dreams, and the product of an illusion. There is not a spark of spiritual energy discoverable in him. His language appears to belong to a certain tribe of monkeys inhabiting the dark and impenetrable continent that lies beyond the confines of our kingdom, where all sorts of hobgoblins, devils, and monsters exist, whose greatest pleasure it is to torture each other. Among them you will find different degrees of insanity: they wander about in the dark, without knowing from whence they came or what will be the end of their journey; turning around in a circular dance, sometimes whirling in one direction and then again in another, always returning to the place from which they started, without making any progress. Nevertheless, some of them are said to enjoy their condition, because they do not know anything better. They do not know their own selves, and they are not alive; they only dream that they live, and mistake their dreams for realities. Some of them may even dream to be men. They are dreams in a dream. They have their imaginary dream-knowledge, dream-pleasures, and dream-sorrows, and imagine them to be real. After a certain time they evaporate."

     The comet-drivers

Something in Cravatu's manner made me feel that there was a grain of truth in what he said, and kept me from getting angry; but I did not like to hear a gnome speaking so disrespectfully of the human race. I therefore said—

"I beg pardon. The place which you describe may be Purgatory or something worse, but not our world, in which it is, after all, very pleasant to live. We are neither fools nor idiots, but we have among us people of great learning, scientists and inventors, and we have many things which are quite beyond the power of the comprehension of a gnome."

"Listen to that phantom!" exclaimed Cravatu. "How every word of his confirms what I said. It would be impossible to convince the product of a delusion that he is only an illusion, because, believing himself to be real, all his delusions seem real to him. Not knowing their own real self, but only what appears to be their self, they do not perceive anything real, but see only that which appears to be, and never that which really is."

Upon this a general discussion took place. Some of the gnomes expressed their opinion that I might be a man after all without knowing it; others said that they perceived that I was only a spook; some thought I was a cheat, and others expressed their belief that I was the product of an auto-suggestion. At last some of the brightest gnomes held a consultation together, and when it was ended, one of the wisest-looking came up to me and said—

"We will allow you fair play. Men are all-knowing, and, if you are a man, you will be able to answer a question. Will you therefore have the kindness to tell us what is the cube-root of the diameter of a circle having a periphery of 3,1415, if you please?"

This of course I did not know, and therefore I said—

"I am not a mathematician, and you will therefore have to ask me something easier. But, even if I were an expert in mathematics, I would require a piece of paper and a pencil to figure it out."

This remark of mine caused a great deal of merriment among all the gnomes present. They jumped and yelled, and punching each others' ribs with the tips of their fingers, they cried—

"Ho! Ho! He does not know the cube-root of the diameter of a circle having a periphery of 3,1415," and from every corner of the place, where groups of gnomes were standing, and from every projecting rock, where some of them were perching and listening, shouts of derisive laughter came back, repeating the suggestive and exasperating words: "Ho! Ho! He does not know the cube-root of the diameter of a circle having a periphery of 3,1415."

"This is very idiotic!" I cried. "How could anybody know anything without figuring it out or being informed about it?"

A triumphant smile appeared upon Cravatu's face, and Adalga looked downcast and perplexed, but my remarks only increased the hilarity of the gnomes, many of whom stood upon their heads, and swinging their legs, roared—

"He sees nothing! He knows nothing! He imagines to know what he is informed about! He knows nothing himself!"

In the midst of this uproar a blast of trumpets was heard. Order was immediately restored, and the gnomes whispered to each other—

"The king!"

A sound as of many tinkling silver bells announced the arrival of his majesty, and immediately afterwards I saw a globe of red light of unusual size, accompanied by many smaller ones approaching, and directly I stood in the presence of Bimbam I., king of the gnomes.

The king, whenever he condescended to assume a corporeal form, appeared as a gnome of noble bearing, medium-sized, and of middle age, having a yellow beard, while upon his head rested a crown with many stars; the greatest of them being a large carbuncle, emitting a living red light, which enveloped his person, and caused everything upon which it radiated to appear in a red colour.

"What is all this row about?" asked the king. "Has Kalutho again forgotten to collect electricity from the clouds, and to supply with vitality the roots of the buttercups on the eastern side of the mountain?"

"Worse than that, your Majesty," replied Cravatu, saluting the king. "A spectre from the country of dreams has dared to penetrate into your kingdom, and it remains with your majesty to decide what is to be done with it. It is an animal hobgoblin belonging to the third dimension of space."

Thus speaking, he handed to the king the spiritoscope, through which Bimbam I. took a long look at me, and returning it to the minister, he spoke only one word—

"Empty!"

"What is most curious about it, if your majesty will permit," continued Cravatu, "is that this three-dimensional apparition dreams that it is one of those supernatural beings which once existed upon the earth and were called men!"

Upon hearing these words the king broke out into such a roar of laughter that it was fearful to behold. He held his sides and laughed so that it shook the rocks and disintegrated some of them, while all the gnomes laughed with him. When the noise had subsided, Cravatu again spoke and said—

"If it pleases your majesty to observe that the semi-intellectual forces in nature produce such elemental forms. They do nothing by their own volition, but act only according to the influences which act upon them. Anybody can make them do as he pleases."

So saying, Cravatu made a sign to one of the gnomes,

whom I afterwards learned to know as Clavo, the commanding
general of the army. He was a robust fellow, and very quick.
Before I knew what he was about, he drew a pin, which he
carried in a scabbard by his side, and stuck it into my back. I
cried out, and made a jump.

"It is evident," said the king, "that he is an elemental.
Spirits do not squeal and jump when they are stuck with a pin."

This remark annoyed me, and I howled—

"I do not claim to be a spirit; I only said that I am a man!"

His majesty grinned ironically.

"Who ever heard," he said, "of a real man who is not a
spirit?"

Cravatu then motioned to another gnome who carried a
fiddle under his arm, and that fellow, understanding the order,
began to play a jig. I am a great lover of music, and love to
dance, and this surely was the best Irish jig I ever listened to;
but I did not want to make an exhibition of myself before the
king, and resisted the impulse. At last, however, the music
got the best of me, my legs began to jerk, and before I really
knew what I was doing, I danced the jig as lively as I ever
danced one in my life.

"He dreams that he is a man," said the king, "but he is only
a product of nature. If you stick his body with a pin, it jumps;
if you fiddle to his legs, he dreams that he must dance. I do
not perceive any spirit nor anything supernatural in him; he is
only a composition of semi-intelligent forces of nature. One
can make such a compound do what one likes. We can make
it amiable or disagreeable, gay or sorry, angry or contented,
envious or generous, jealous, furious, or whatever one likes."

While the king spoke these words, the princess gave a faint
cry, and as I looked at her I saw that the silvery white of her
star had assumed a bluish tint. This was noticed by all the
gnomes, and they became very much alarmed.

"Her royal highness, the princess, has fallen in love," cried Cravatu, in a sorrowful tone, and the king quickly replied—

"Let the physician of the court be summoned immediately."

These words were hardly spoken when the doctor made his appearance. He was an old fellow, with a benevolent expression, wearing a blue cape with yellow borders. He had a grey beard, and wore a pair of golden spectacles.

Unlike our doctors, he did not ask the patient any questions; he did not feel her pulse, nor even look at her tongue; but, like all gnomes, he knew things by direct perception, and saw immediately what was the matter with her. Turning to the king he expressed his sorrow that such an unfortunate accident should have happened to a member of the royal family, and for the purpose of removing the cause of the disease, he advised the king that the object of the affection of the princess—meaning myself—should have his head sawed off immediately.

To my horror, Adalga consented cheerfully, and the king was about to give the required order, when the doctor spoke again, and said—

"If her royal highness would consent to wait until the next night, I would propose to preserve the subject, and instead of sawing its head off, have it dissected alive in the presence of the medical faculty, as it would be very interesting to our physiologists to see of what material spooks are made. If the princess would consent to have that much patience, the whole profession would be thankful to her."

The princess declared herself willing to wait, and said that the sensation she experienced was rather pleasant that painful to her. Thereupon the king said in a stern manner—

"See that he does not escape. Put him under the jumping-jack!" So saying, the king and his suite turned to go.

"The jumping-jack!"—what a horror crept over me when

I heard these terrible words. My frame began to tremble, and my hair stood on one end at the very thought of this jumping-jack, although I had not the faintest idea of what it was, but imagined it to be some instrument of torture. Soon, however, I had my doubts cleared up; for the head executioner, a strong fellow in a scarlet robe, together with his attendants, brought forth the instrument. It consisted of a yellow stick, upon which a wooden monkey, painted purple, was with its hands attached to a movable crossbar at the top, leaving the body free to climb up and down. This they placed before me, planting the stick into the ground, and by means of some contrivance unknown to me, they set the wooden monkey a-going, and quietly walked away, leaving me alone with the princess.

I do not know how it came, but that wooden monkey exerted a powerful influence over me. I had often seen such jumping-jacks at toy-shops, but never experienced such an attraction before. I could not divert my eyes from that monkey. I called myself a thousand times a fool for paying any attention at all to a jumping-jack, and nevertheless it kept me spell-bound. I could do nothing else but sit there with my eyes rivetted upon that monkey. I knew that the princess was still with me, and I heard her imploring me with tears, by all that was sacred to me, to desist from paying attention to that jumping-jack.

"Dearest Mulligan!" she cried, "why will you not desist from worshipping that monkey? Why will you not make love to me? See, the doors are open, and there is nothing to hinder us to depart. Have I not promised you to follow you wherever you go?"

"Let me alone!" I cried in rage. "I cannot take my eyes away from that confounded jack."

"Is this your manhood?" continued Adalga, weeping and wringing her hands. "Are you a supernatural being, and the sight of a monkey can make you forget yourself and your

     The comet-drivers

promises? Is this your love and affection for me, which a purple monkey can steal away? O Mulligan! Mulligan! leave off looking at that jumping-jack and remember your duty! Come into my arms!"

"I wish that confounded hypnotism had never been invented!" I cried; but for all that I was not able to break the spell. The princess kept on crying bitterly, and begging me to desist. I heard her speak, but what she said had no effect upon me. What did I care for a princess, while I enjoyed the sight of that dear jumping-jack? I knew that if I did not control myself I would have to remain in this situation and be tortured to death at the appointed hour; but what was that to me? I cared for nothing else but for the sight of that monkey in whom all my affections were centred. I thought of the princess with entire indifference. Oh, how I loved that jumping-jack! It was as dear to me as if it had been my own self. I could not think of anything but of that jumping-jack, and I involuntarily hummed the song in which my situation was so well portrayed by the words of a well-known poet:—

"Willie had a purple monkey

Climbing on a yellow stick."

It never occurred to me to lick off the paint. I knew nothing more. I was asleep, with the jumping-jack in my arms.

IV
AMONG THE GNOMES

Hypnotized by a Monkey

WHILE I was sleeping I experienced a horrible dream. The jumping-jack before me assumed the features of a baboon, having a great resemblance to Professor Cracker, and besides this there were two grotesque figures standing at the foot of the pole. One was wooden nut-cracker with goggle eyes, a long nose and protruding chin, the very image of Jeremiah Stiffbone; and the other a curiously shaped whisky-jug of stoneware, having the form and features of Mr Scalawag; and while the monkey was moving up and down on the pole, the nut-cracker and the whisky-jug danced, and all three sang the following song:

Huzza and hey-day! Up and down we go;

There being nothing that we do not know.

We prove that black is white and white is black,

And all the world admires the jumping-jack.

And as we jump go jumping all the rest;

Who jumps the highest knows his business best.

Forward and backward on the beaten track:

There's nothing greater than a jumping-jack.

And to our stick we cling from first to last;

Who asks for more is only a fantast.

Thus up and down we go, upward and back:

This is the glory of a jumping-jack.

After they finished singing, the nut-cracker sniffed the air with his nose and turned his goggle eyes in the direction where I was hidden, after which his jaws began to move, and he said:

"I am smelling human flesh. There is some one present."

To this the whisky-jug replied, while grinning from ear to ear:

"Who knows but it may be Mr Schneider, or his ghost."

"Mr Schneider has no ghost," said the baboon. "If we were to find one, we would have to destroy it immediately, to save the reputation of science."

"I am quite sure that something of that kind is hidden somewhere," replied the nut-cracker, and turning to the baboon, he asked: "Do you see anything?"

"Seeing is deceptive," answered the baboon, "but we will see whether we cannot reason it out. Wait till I come down."

So saying, the monkey stopped his motions, and to my horror I saw him unfastening his hands from the crossbar. Climbing down the yellow stick, he joined the whisky-jug and the nut-cracker, and all three searched the place and almost stumbled over me, but they did not see me.

"There is nothing," said the baboon. "However, there can be no doubt that Schneider is dead, and the only thing to be regretted about it is that he did not die in the interest of science. If we had known that he was going to die anyhow, we might have subjected him to certain experiments."

Strange to say, during this dream I had no thought of being a Mulligan; but my individuality was changed back to Mr Schneider. When I awoke Schneider was gone, and I was once more Mulligan.

"De mortuis nil nisi bene!" drawled out the nut-cracker. "But if Schneider had died in the interest of science, it would have been the first useful thing he ever did." So saying, the nut-cracker clapped his jaws.

The whisky-jug blinked with his little eyes and added, "He meant well, but——"

I knew what he was going to say, and this made me very angry. I therefore jumped at him and gave him a box on the ear; but my fist went quite through his head, and it had no other effect upon him than stopping his sentence. He did not seem to notice it; but I now knew that I had died and become a spirit. I also saw that I could take possession of people and use their organs of speech, and as the nut-cracker was nearest to me, I went inside of him and caused him to exclaim:—

"I will show you whether or not I am a well-meaning fool! Confound you and your science! I have been among the gnomes and know that they exist! but you are the blind fools who cannot see anything because you are too stupid to open your eyes."

"Brother Stiffbone has become insane," said the baboon; "let us tie him before he does us any injury."

Thereupon the baboon and the whisky-jug went for me while I was in the nut-cracker's body, and I went in that shape for them. I snapped at the baboon's ear and gave him a black eye, and I tore out a handful of hair from the head of the whisky-jug, who in his turn broke my—that is to say, the nut-cracker's nose. At last they got the best of me; because the wooden limbs of the nut-cracker were so stiff and I could not move them quickly enough. We fell down, and the baboon was kneeling upon my breast when I awoke.

Once more I was Mr Mulligan. I opened my eyes and found myself in inky darkness. The first thing I did was to feel my nose to see whether it was broken. The nose was all right, and its solidity convinced me that I was no ghost, and my adventure with the nut-cracker's body, however real it seemed, had been only a dream. I groped about for the purpose of finding the jumping-jack, but it was gone; neither did I regret its absence, for with the sight of it all my affection for it had departed, and I could not understand how I could have been so foolish as to permit myself to be attracted by it. My desire for the purple monkey had left me; but my love for the princess returned. I yearned for her presence and called her name; but no answer came; there was nothing around me but darkness and solitude.

Ever since that event I have often asked myself, Why do we hate to be for a long time alone? The only answer I could find is, that when we are alone with ourselves, the company of our self is not sufficiently satisfactory and agreeable to us. Perhaps we do not sufficiently know that self to fully enjoy its presence. Perhaps we do not know that self at all, and then of course we are in company with something we do not know, which means in company with nothing, and to enjoy the presence of nothing is to have no enjoyment at all.

I confess that I never realised my own nothingness so much as on that occasion. The old doubts returned again. I did not know whether I was living or whether something which imagined itself to be "I" seemed to live, and if that which only seemed to be myself was to be vivisected, why should I trouble myself about it, as the vivisection of something unknown to me did not concern me at all, unless I voluntarily chose to take any interest in it? But how could I think of making any choice at all if that "I" was something unknown? I instinctively refused to recognise as myself that personality which was governed by the spell of a jumping-jack, and I spoke to myself as if I were another person.

"Well, Mulligan!" I said, "how could you be such an idiot as to submit yourself to the power of a baboon! Really, I doubt whether you are a man. Pshaw! the gnomes are right. You are a monkey yourself, and even inferior to a monkey, because the baboon was your master. A nice lord of creation you are, being controlled by the creation of your own foolish fancy. A lord of creation, indeed! One who cannot even resist the attraction of a jumping-jack!"

Thus I went on moralising, and wondered what my real Ego was, and whether it had anything at all to do with what seemed to be myself. I wished to know whether I—that is to say, my real self—was; for what purpose I was in the world, and where I had been before I entered the world, and what that was which caused me to be born, and whether I would be born again after I—that is to say, my body—had been dissected. Alas, for all these questions Cracker's science had no answer to give, and I envied the gnomes who had the ability to dissolve and condense into bodies at will.

The darkness was very oppressive, and I wished that I could be self-luminous like a gnome, and not be dependent upon an external light for the purpose of seeing. I wondered whether, perhaps, after the dissection of my body, my spirit would have a light of its own, or whether Bimbam was right when he pronounced the suggestive word, "Empty!" Then something, of which I do not know what it was, made me think that the worst thing anybody could possibly do was to doubt or deny the presence of a spiritual light within himself, and while I studied as to what may be that which made me think so, I came to the conclusion that it was my own spirit reminding me of its presence, and this was a more convincing proof to me that I actually had a spirit than all the arguments offered to the contrary by Professor Cracker and his ilk.

With this conviction a great deal of calmness and satisfaction came over me. At the same time the darkness grew less in intensity; a silvery mist, tinged with blue, arose like the dawn that precedes the rising sun; the light grew stronger and condensed in a luminous ball, and the next instant the princess stood before me.

"Dearest Adalga!" I said, "where have you been so long, and why did you leave me alone in this horrible darkness?"

To this the princess answered, "Truth never departs, but error always attracts us. Never for an instant have I deserted you; I was with you and around you all the time, but you kept your eyes closed and refused to see."

"On the contrary," I replied, "I strained my eyes to look through the darkness, but there was nothing."

"You strained your eyes," answered the princess, "for the purpose of seeing my form, which was not formed, and which could not be seen; but you made no effort to see that which is without form, but which may be seen with the inner eye. Know, my beloved, that when you see my form you do not see me, and when you do not see my form you may see me in truth."

"This," I said, "is contrary to all the doctrines of our science, which teaches that we can see nothing whatever unless it has a shape of some kind."

"The eye of science sees only the outward form," answered Adalga; "but the eye of wisdom sees the reality itself."

"I understand," I replied. "I have learned a lesson, and henceforth the delusion caused by forms shall have no more power over me. But tell me, dear, is the hour of vivisection approaching? Is there no way for escape?"

"Alas, no!" sighed the princess. "There is a jumping-jack at every door."

A thrill of horror swept through me when I heard these words, and made me tremble. A moment before I had called myself a fool for being afraid of a jumping-jack, and now at the very mention of such a toy the old terror came back. I knew that I could not escape, because I would not dare to face a jumping-jack again. I would be sure to succumb to its influence.

"But," continued Adalga, "why should you be afraid of being dissected? Can you not create for yourself a new body again?"

"Nonsense!" I cried. "I am not a creator."

"But, sure enough," answered the princess, "you have a creative spirit in you. Oh, my dear Mulligan, why will you remain incognito among us? Why do you continue to be dark? Why will you disguise yourself before me? Is it that I am not worthy to behold your true light, or that my eyes would be dazzled by its splendour? Lord of my heart, unveil yourself to me! Show yourself to me in your own essence!"

"Dearest princess!" I replied, "I do not know what you are talking about. I am not luminous, and I never saw a luminous man. In our country nobody has a light of his own."

"Alas!" said the princess, "what a fearful fate it must be to have no light, and to live in a country of perpetual darkness."

To this I replied—

"This is not so. Nobody in our country needs a light of his own, because we have one great luminary, called the sun, right over our head, and the light of that sun illuminates our world."

"And can everybody see that sun?" asked the princess.

"Of course," I said. "Everybody, unless he is as blind as a bat."

When I had spoken these words, the princess threw her arms around my neck, and whispered to me—

"Dearest Mulligan! I have a favour to ask you. Please fetch me the sun!"

"This is quite impossible," I said, "for although we all live in the light of the sun, nevertheless we cannot approach the sun, nor put him into our pockets."

But the princess was not satisfied with that answer. "Surely,"

 The comet-drivers

she exclaimed, "you told me that the sun was right above your heads. You ought not to refuse me the first kindness I ever asked of you. I implore you to bring me the sun. I will not be contented unless I have it."

I became alarmed. "This is a foolish request, madame," I said. "If somebody, or anybody, could claim the sun as his own, and carry it away, there would be little chance for anyone else to enjoy it. The Government would monopolise it, and put a tax upon the use of his light; the doctors would dissect him to see of what material he is made; and there are lots of amorous fools who would not hesitate a moment to make him explode, merely for the purpose of amusing their sweethearts."

But it was of no use to argue such a thing with a being unacquainted with the first rules of logic, and the princess went on with tears and sobs to beg me to fetch her the sun. I tried my best to explain to her the absurdity of the request, but she would not listen; and, weeping bitterly, she cried—

"O Mulligan, you do not love me! Is this your gratitude for bestowing my affection upon you?"

I felt very miserable, and began to look upon myself as the most ungrateful wretch, and to appease her I promised that I would try to do all I could.

At this moment a blast of trumpets and the tinkling of bells announced the arrival of the king. He was accompanied by the queen and her suite, and with them came all the nobility, the ministers, officers, and also the whole of the medical faculty, together with the head executioner and his assistants. The queen was a little fat woman, and rather homely. Upon her head shone a great emerald, throwing a soft green light around her. She was accompanied by her maids of honour, all of whom appeared in a green colour.

I made my bow to the queen, who, after looking at me through the spiritoscope, turned to the king and said—

"Is this the green hobgoblin who has the impudence of

claiming that he is a man-spirit?"

"Yes," answered the king; "only, as you will observe, he is not green, but red."

"Your majesty is pleased to jest," replied the queen. "Everybody sees that he is green."

"He is red," said the king sternly, being evidently annoyed by her contradiction.

"Let him be red then, if you must have it so," answered the queen, while her voice indicated vexation; "but he is green for all that."

"Well, I declare!" exclaimed Bimbam I., growing still more red. "I never saw a woman in my life that did not love to contradict. I say he is red, and I will leave it to Cravatu to decide."

Cravatu stepped forward, letting his yellow light fall directly upon me, and after scanning me very carefully, he said: "I beg pardon, your majesties, but the hobgoblin is of a bright yellow colour."

"Are you all making sport of me?" cried the king in a rage; and turning to the princess, he asked: "What does Adalga say?"

"He appears to me in a silvery light shaded with blue," answered the princess; "but according to his own statement he does not shine at all."

The gnomes looked at each other in amazement, and Cravatu said—

"He is a wizard who appears to everyone in another light."

But the princess continued—

"Although he does not shine, he has a much greater light than we all, for it shines upon everything. He calls it a sun, and he has promised to fetch it to me."

Therefore the king ordered that I should immediately show

him the sun, and when I succeeded in making him understand that it could not be removed from its place in the universe, and that the only way of convincing oneself of its existence was to step within the sphere of its light, the king ordered Cravatu to select immediately a committee of three of the most clever gnomes for the purpose of going to the country of dreams and to hunt for the sun.

Accordingly three gnomes of rank were selected. They were of a white colour, and the light that radiated from them was so brilliant that it dazzled one's eyes to look at it. They immediately assumed their spherical shapes and floated away; but the king ordered that my execution should be stayed until after their discovery of the sun.

When I heard these words I felt much relieved in my mind, for I had now some hope of escape.

"May your majesty persevere in that resolution!" I said to the king. "For these three messengers will never discover the sun. They have too splendid lights of their own to be able to see beyond it. They will be dazzled and blinded by their own radiance, and not look for the light of the sun."

Upon hearing these words everybody seemed highly astonished. The gnomes looked at each other in surprise, and whispered: "He is a prophet! He can foretell future events! This is quite supernatural!"

"It does not require any supernatural power," I said, "to be able to foretell that a thing cannot take place, on account of its being impossible. Everybody knows that a certain amount of darkness is required for the purpose of enabling one to perceive light. Those who are full of their own light cannot see the light of another, just as those who love to hear only themselves talking will not listen to what another one says."

"Wonderful!" exclaimed the king, and Cravatu whispered to him: "He is one of those who see what is not."

But I continued saying: "If your majesty wishes to obtain

information regarding the existence of truth, I would advise you to send a committee of such as are less conceited and capable of seeing beyond the wall which their egoism has built around them."

I was still speaking when the three gnomes returned, and they reported unanimously that they had been to dreamland, and that they had seen no other light but their own, and that it was an absurdity to believe in the existence of a universal sun; for if there were such a light it could not have escaped their notice, and, moreover, the presence of such a light would make everybody look of the same colour, so that not one person could be distinguished from another.

Thereupon all the dark gnomes, such as had as little light and intelligence as possible, were gathered, and out of them the king selected three almost entirely dark dwarfs. They were surely the most sorry-looking imbeciles which it has ever been my misfortune to behold. Big-headed, hydrocephalic, with shrunken brains, they were the very personification of abject stupidity; they seemed to have not more understanding than an oyster, although their power of seeing appeared good enough. These were appointed as a committee to seek for the sun, and it was ordered that they should be conducted to the frontier of the outer world, there to be left to their own fate and to begin their researches. This was accordingly done: the three idiots were taken away, and I pitied them, for I doubted whether they would ever have sense enough to find their way back.

"I am curious to hear the report of this committee," remarked the queen, "perhaps it would have been still better to blindfold them."

To this I replied—

"I fear that your majesty will be disappointed; for, even if the dwarfs perceive the sun, they will be incapable to understand what they see, or to describe it."

"Hear! hear!" exclaimed the king, and all the gnomes

began to regard me with awe and respect; but Cravatu said—

"Really there is more behind this person than we suspected. He is one of those who sees that which cannot be."

Thereupon the king conferred upon me the office of head fortune-teller to the court, and I was treated with great respect. The whole behaviour of the gnomes changed; the queen smiled at me, and invited me to the palace; but the princess was delighted, and as she took my arm, she said to me with a triumphant smile: "I knew that you were more than a spook after all."

V
AMONG THE GNOMES

(continued)

THE DISCOVERY OF THE SUN

WE arrived at the king's palace, a description of which will undoubtedly interest the reader, and I only regret my inability to do full justice to this subject.

The palace consisted of an extensive building of white alabaster upon a rose-coloured marble foundation, and with a gilded dome-shaped roof over the main portion of the building, while the adjoining parts were shaped in various ways. The whole represented a mixture of Grecian and Moorish styles; there was a high portal whose columns were of white marble with veins of gold. Entering through the main door we came into a spacious courtyard, filled with works of art, representing antediluvian monstrosities of the various ages of the world. There we saw the Ichthyosaurus, Plesiosaurus, and Megatherium, and similar animals unknown in history; enormous snakes, turtles, and crocodiles, in what is supposed to have been their original size and shape, and besides these there were represented such failures of nature as may have existed in the earliest time of the world's history— women with fish-tails, human bodies with animal heads, and animal bodies with human heads or limbs, fauns, mermaids, satyrs, centaurs, flying snakes, dragons, etc. Curiously enough, the gnomes claimed that these were the representations of their ancestors, and they paid great respect to them. This courtyard extended all around the palace, surrounding it like a ring.

From this court we entered into an entrance hall built of yellow stone, at the door of which were standing two gigantic umbrella-shaped mushrooms of scarlet colour with white filaments, resembling the finest kind of lace.

This hall was exquisitely furnished and ornamented with various mushrooms, all of an edible kind, affording at once comfort and food; for while resting upon a lounge or sitting at a table, if one wanted to eat, all he had to do was to eat a piece of the furniture. There was the Agaricus deliciosus, procerus, campestris, prunulus, Boletus edulis, Polyporus confluens, Hydrum repandum and imbriatum, the Clavaria Botrytis, Morchella esculenta, Helvella crispa, Bovista nigrescens, and many others, whose names I have forgotten, and still others which even Professor Cracker has not yet classified. They were serving either as tables, couches, or chairs; and there was not a single toadstool or poisonous fungus among them. There were no chandeliers, lamps, or candlesticks of any kind, for the gnomes lived in a natural manner and needed no artificial lights. Each gnome was himself a light more or less luminous according to the degree of his or her intelligence. But to me, having no light of my own and no power to illuminate anything, it was a source of continual annoyance that I always needed the company of some gnome to keep me enlightened, as otherwise I would have been left in utter darkness and nothingness. Moreover, the light in which a thing appeared to me always depended on the colour of the light of this or that gnome who happened to be in my presence, which caused me to experience a continual change of opinions regarding the qualities of the objects I saw.

From this hall a flight of seven marble steps led into the main building of the palace. This consisted of eight divisions, each made of a different quality; while the whole was built in a star-shaped form; so that each division with its sub-divisions was connected directly with the central chamber occupied by the king. But what was most curious about it was, that in each division some special invisible genii or spirit seemed to preside; for in each a peculiar influence differing from the rest could be felt by anyone whose nerves were not made of cast-iron or who was not a blockhead.

Thus the hall of the mushrooms on the north side breathed an air of luxury and enjoyment; while the room to the left of it was pervaded by a spirit of anxiety and dissatisfaction, and was visited only by those who by force of habit had become attracted to it, and who, so to say, found satisfaction only in being always dissatisfied; chronic grumblers, misanthropes, people discontented with themselves and with everything. On the other hand, there were two rooms to the east, in which nobody could remain without being overcome by a feeling of awe, reverence, generosity, sublimity, and a deep religious sentiment. They were visited by the brightest of the gnomes, and served as places for contemplation. These rooms seemed to be empty, but they were not empty; because, while they were bare of all objects, they were filled with an overwhelming abundance of that spirit which is the creator or producer of forms.

The south-eastern portion of the palace contained the sleeping apartments of the royal family, and whoever entered there would sink into a state of torpor and forgetfulness; but the hall next to that, lying directly towards the south, inspired its inhabitants with a deep melancholy easily turned into anger. Another division towards the west was called the chamber of cunning, and used on certain occasions for the purpose of concocting schemes of revenge and intrigue. It was very seldom used at the time of my arrival, but became a favourite meeting-room later on. As to the hall upon the north side, which was dedicated to all sorts of sensual enjoyment, it was

 The comet-drivers

The Place of the King

the most attractive, but also the most dangerous of them all, and I am bound by promise not to divulge any of its mysteries.

All these rooms were free of access to every gnome of good standing; but the division in the centre, where the king resided, was open only to those who gained admission there. It was always guarded by a selected number of female soldiers, corresponding to our Amazons, and it was said that female soldiers were always chosen in preference, because they were more faithful and reliable than the males among the gnomes.

At the entrance of the king's chamber there were statues of gigantic size, reminding me of the ones at the British Museum which were brought there from Easter Island. They represented that prehistoric race of beings which the gnomes used to call "Man," or "Homo divinus," and of which they claimed that it existed no more upon the planet earth, having emigrated to other spheres, and abandoned their country to hobgoblins, devils, and spooks. I must confess that in our country I never met with any human beings of such a superhuman aspect as was represented here. There were images of men and women of such noble mien and so awe-inspiring, that they looked much more like gods than like specimens of the genus homo bipex, and a resemblance to them can be found only among the statuary of the ancient Greeks. Here the king in person resided, and nobody dared to approach him without his consent, and without being admitted by the Amazons; but the apartments of the princess were next to those of the king, and as I spent a great deal of time in her company, I also came very frequently in contact with her father the king.

The most remarkable thing among the gnomes was that they could not distinguish falsehood from truth. They were incapable of saying anything else than what they themselves thought and believed, and they could not conceive of the possibility of telling a lie. This state of affairs was sometimes somewhat annoying, for it is not always agreeable to hear some one state his opinion about you right to your face; but on the other hand it was advantageous in many respects. For instance, whenever I wanted to enter the chamber of the king, all I had to do was to tell the Amazons that the king wanted to see me; and I believe if anyone had told the treasurer of the kingdom that he was entitled to take the treasure away, the guardian would have delivered it up without hesitation. This, however, was only at the time of my arrival, and before an attempt of civilising the gnomes was made. Time passed away rapidly, and I do not know how long I remained at the palace enjoying the hospitality of the queen and the company of the princess; but each day I learned more to admire Adalga's character; the simplicity of her way of thinking, and the purity of her affection. It is true that her want of modern education, her inability to hide her true sentiments, and her inexperience in the habits of modern civilisation—especially in what refers to conventionalities—sometimes created a feeling of dissatisfaction in my mind. She did not know how to pretend sentiments which she did not experience; she knew nothing about logical quibbles and tergiversation, nor of the many sweet little lies that make life supportable among mankind. It never occurred to her to say anything just for the sake of using a little flattery or tickling one's vanity, or for the purpose of teasing; and of all such things which are much admired among people of culture she knew nothing. This I regretted, but I could not keep myself from admiring her naturalness and sincerity. We passed a great deal of our time in the hall at the north end, and the princess asked me a thousand questions in regard to the constitution, customs and habits of the human kingdom, the manners of its inhabitants, their object of living and occupation, and the immortality of their souls.

"I know, love of my heart!" she used to say, "that if I could only become fully identified with you, we would both be as one immortal being, and it is only the dark aspect of your nature which prevents this unification and identity."

"But why, dearest one!" I asked, "can you not become immortal without this unification that would destroy your identity? Have you not within yourself all the elements necessary for that purpose?"

"Alas, no!" answered the princess. "These elements are within us, but they are capable of development only in the constitution of man, and therefore we strive to become human just as you strive to become gods. But the race of real human beings has disappeared, and only a spurious imitation is left. These are the ghosts and hobgoblins with whom intercourse is forbidden, and we are now doomed to be left for ages without any prospect of real progress, until a race of real men appears again upon the earth."

I answered her questions as well as I could, assuring her that there were still a great many honest and noble-minded people among what she called hobgoblins and ghosts, and that they would be glad to contract marriages with gnomes and sylphs, if they knew that they could thereby be useful to them. I said that there were among us millions of people who did not know that they were immortal, but that thousands of clergymen were engaged in the occupation of making them believe it. I also said that new systems of ethics, morals, and philosophy were being invented almost every day, and that the world of humanity would soon become very much improved.

"Oh, I wish I were a man!" exclaimed Adalga.

"This will be impossible in your present incarnation," I said. "But I will do all I can to develop in you a human mind and teach you all that men know."

"Oh, do please!" cried the princess, embracing me in the exuberance of her joy.

"First of all," I said, "you must learn the rules of logic, syntax and induction, illation, postulation, assumption and inference. You must learn to doubt everything you see and feel, and deny all you hear. Never believe anything unless you already know all the whys and wherefores, and never take anything for granted unless it comes from an authority which you believe to be respectable, and which is recognised as such by the crowd. Deny everything that you do not understand, consider everybody a liar until he has irrefutably proved his veracity; never let anybody get the advantage of you by showing yourself to him such as you are, and never do anything without getting a personal profit."

I stopped, because I saw that these maxims were all gibberish to the princess, and that she did not understand what I said; but I resolved to try my best to instruct her, and to bring intellectual culture among the gnomes.

During these happy days, and while waiting for the return of the three imbeciles, I highly enjoyed the novelty of my situation. My liberty was not restricted, and I had ample opportunity for studying the character and the habits of the gnomes, in which occupation I was liberally aided by the princess. Arm in arm we wandered or floated through the villages, visited the mines and observed the gnomes at their labour, and I was astonished at the untold amount of treasures in the Untersberg, the existence of which is little suspected.

The gnomes on the whole were at that time an unsophisticated lot; because, owing to their simple nature, a gnome could only think one thought at a time. They were therefore not given to reasoning and argumentation, and lived fully contented. In fact, they were rather deficient in intellectuality, but in spite of that, or perhaps on account of it, they had a great deal of spiritual power. Falsehood, lying, hypocrisy, scheming, and wilful deception were unknown to them, and as stated above, they always meant what they said, and took it for granted that everyone except a hobgoblin or spook meant what his words implied; nor would it have been possible for a gnome to tell a wilful lie without experiencing therefrom immediately a detrimental effect upon his constitution; for as it was the light of truth that made them luminous, the telling of a falsehood, or even the thinking of one, would have immediately diminished the amount of his or her luminosity, which would have at once become visible to the rest; or it might have extinguished their light for ever. Thus they were, by the necessity of their nature, always open and sincere, and followed their impulses for good or evil without being guided by the reasoning intellect.

Whatever was done by them was done in good faith, even if it was foolish; there never was any malicious intent.

Being capable of perceiving the truth directly and without reasoning, by the power of pure reason or instinct, they could solve the most difficult mathematical problems by merely looking at the final result, and nearly every one of them could thus have made a fortune among us by giving exhibitions of his power as a mathematical phenomenon, without the least knowledge of mathematics; but they could not even make the smallest calculation or draw any inferences from given factors. They knew what they knew because they perceived it, and there was no guessing about what they saw.

I found them to be exceedingly impressible by my thoughts and emotions. I often amused myself with the lower orders of gnomes by making them act out what I thought. When I, for instance, imagined myself to be afraid of them, they would become immediately afraid of me and run away. When I became angry at them, they became angry at me, even if I said not a word nor showed it by my manners. I think that if I had secretly determined to kill a gnome, he would have unknowingly followed the impulse and killed me. This made me think of the story of Burkhart of Tollenstein, and that perhaps many suicides may be thus due to the ire aroused in those semi-intelligent forces of nature which we find objectified in the kingdom of gnomes.

There was one class of gnomes called Pigmies, whose office it was to direct the currents of vital electricity in the earth to all places where the roots of the plants that grew upon the surface required it. This they did while they were in their disembodied state, when each of them was, so to say, like a magnetic current; but whenever they assumed corporeal forms they were very small, and perhaps for this reason they had a dislike against appearing in corporeal bodies, and did so only for the purpose of taking food, or for some other

    The comet-drivers

object which required material organs. They were composed of some substantial but bodiless active force, which they could cause to crystallise into a nucleus of latent energy. In such a condition they were very lazy; but when liberated they were very active. They were strong, and it was surprising to see what an amount of active force could be developed from a comparatively insignificant spark of energy.

Next, there were the Vulcani, who were principally occupied with mineral life, having in their charge the growth and transformation of metals. Their substance consisted of a certain force for which we have no name, but which might be called an electro-magnetic fire. By an exercise of their will they were able to send a current of such vital electricity into a mineral vein, and cause gold and silver, iron and copper, to grow; for it is a sign of short-sightedness if one believes that metals have no life and do not grow, because their growth is not so rapid and perceptible as that of the plants.

Then there were the Cubitali, and the substance of which they were formed was a kind of explosive force, which means that they could contract their fluidic bodies and expand them very rapidly, when the quick expansion caused a kind of explosion with a destructive effect. Whenever they assumed a form they were about two feet high, well built, and showing great muscular strength. They were, so to say, the hard-working class, and their principal occupation was the blasting of air and the cutting of rocks; and, in spite of their robust appearance, they had a great deal of artistic talent, as was proved by the products of their labour that could be seen in the palace of the king.

Furthermore, there were the Acthnici, constituted of "Acthna," an invisible subterranean fire, who, whenever they manifested themselves in forms and became visible, appeared like fiery globes and balls of lightning. They were, on the whole, stupid and dangerous, and it was said that on more than one occasion some of them had entered dreamland—as they called our world—and been seen by the spooks and returned no more; all of which may, perhaps, have been only a fable, believed only by the children of the gnomes. The Acthnici were said to create heat and cause upheavings of the earth, and some of our ancient philosophers believed them to cause explosions in our mines. However that may be, I never saw them at work, for they were uncouth fellows, and I loved to avoid their society.

There were also the Sagani, and they were the cleverest of all. They were tall and well-formed, resembling the human shape in stature and form whenever they assumed a body. They were from three to five feet high, but they had the power to elongate themselves from the normal size up to a length of twenty-five feet and more. Their principal occupation was to construct the astral models of plants after a certain type for each species, which they did by the power of their imagination (I have no other suitable word); and here I beg to add in parenthesis that, according to my observation among the gnomes, every plant, stone, or tree upon the Untersberg had its "Leffahs," as it is called by the gnomes, or astral type within the astral body of that mountain; each being in some way which I am unable to explain, connected with the physical part of the corresponding organism; so that the physical and (to us) visible product was always the exact image and corporeal representation of its ethereal progenitor and counterpart that is invisible to us but visible to the gnomes.

All the gnomes could at all times and at their own pleasure live in their ethereal states without any definite form, comparable to air or clouds or mists; or they could by an effort of will assume material and corporeal forms, each one according to his or her innate qualities. In their ethereal shape they could travel with the velocity of a thought, and penetrate through the most solid rocks like a current of electricity passing through a bar of iron; but in their corporeal state their locomotion was comparatively slow, and the atmospheric air, not being their own element, caused great obstacles to their locomotion. For the purpose of passing through air, they had to employ cutting and blasting and other methods similar to those which we use for tunnelling rocks.

It is believed by some people that when our bodies are asleep, our spirits are free to roam consciously through space, and experience things which we do not remember when we awake, but which appear to us at best as a dream. Something similar was the case with the gnomes. In their ethereal states they were individual powers, as distinct from each other as electricity is distinct from light, or heat from sound, and as such they were in possession of consciousness and perception of a spiritual kind, and capable of remembering all they had experienced while condensed into a corporeal form. But whenever they assumed corporeal bodies, they had no distinct recollection of what they had been doing while in a state of dissolution, and this was explained to me by the fact that while in their ethereal state their brains were not solidified enough to register and retain the impressions which they received; but the higher impressions which they received while in their corporeal forms they remembered also in their ethereal state, and whenever a gnome entered into the ethereal state he knew all that he had been doing in the same state before. Moreover, there was a state in which they lived in a semi-corporeal and semi-ethereal condition, and this was when they had not fully dissolved their forms, but merely assumed the shape of a globe of light.

From all this it will appear that it is as difficult for a gnome to penetrate into our world as it is for us to penetrate into theirs, and even, as it often may happen, a gnome, while in his incorporeal form, visits mankind, he will not remember anything about it when he returns, or it will appear to him like a dream, and this may be the reason that our world has gained the reputation among the gnomes as being a dreamland,

and nothing more. It may be a dreamland to them as theirs is to us. But they appeared to me to live and exist in their own sphere as much as we in ours. As to the rest, they were born, ate, drank, slept, married, and evaporated after death.

Each family and each tribe of gnomes had its own head and leaders, whom they implicitly obeyed, without even knowing the possibility of disobedience, because they were not given to arguing, and all were ruled by Bimbam I. The administration of the kingdom was very simple; there were no taxes to pay, and everyone had what he wanted, because nobody wanted more than he had. The king took whatever he needed, and never more than he cared to have. Custom-house duties, monopolies, privileges, and corporation nuisances were entirely unknown, and there was no newspaper to disseminate gossip, cause dissensions, and ruin characters for the sake of getting up a sensation. There were no shams. The nobility consisted of gnomes that were truly noble, and not merely pretended to be so; the doctors actually knew something, and did not merely make believe that they were in possession of knowledge; the goodness of the good could be estimated by the amount of light that radiated from their stars, and their character was indicated by the colour of the star. Consequently each individual sphere of light slowly changed when a new emotion or virtue grew in a gnome. Anger made them red, love blue, intelligence yellow, sensuality green, wisdom violet, and so forth.

The ladies of the gnomes occupied positions similar to those of our wives and daughters. The lower classes joined the males in their work; the higher ones were of a more ornamental character, and protectors of arts. The world of gnomes, the same as ours, would have been dreary without female beauty and loveliness. Many of the gnomesses were exceedingly beautiful and ethereal, others were homely; but all of them were very amiable, because they acted in a natural manner, made no attempt of disguising their feelings, and

 The comet-drivers

knew of no such thing as deceit; neither did they disfigure their forms by absurd fashions in dress.

Love-making and wooing were carried on among the gnomes as it is with us, only with the exception that the females had the same right as the males to bestow their affection and to make proposals; neither was it considered a disgrace for any lady to do so; on the contrary, it would have been a disgrace for her to pretend to have other sentiments than she had, and it would have injured her beauty and destroyed her light. There was, however, no such thing as what is understood among us as "women's rights," for their natural instincts taught them that not everything that becomes a male also becomes a female; these gnomes made no attempt to overstep the limits drawn by nature, for this would have caused them to become degraded and unnatural. On account of their simple-mindedness immorality was entirely unknown, because true morality has its basis in the instinctive perception of truth, and requires no artificially concocted systems and shams. One may be very moral without even knowing that moral doctrines exist, and another may know all the moral prescriptions by heart, and be a rascal for all that.

There was one class of females distinguished from the rest. They were such as, having attained a certain age, were still without children. They corresponded to what is in our world called "old maids"; but they were neither old nor ugly. In fact, they were on the whole very charming, and could sing beautiful songs, as everyone knows who has lived for a certain time in the vicinity of the Untersberg, and heard them sing. Their songs are usually of a sad character, and alluring; they express their loneliness and longing for children. The love for production exists in all departments of nature, and also among the gnomes. A gnome having no knowledge of his own, is always happy to stuff his head with theories belonging to others, and loves them as if they were his own children. The same is the case with the so-called "wild women" of the

Untersberg. Their love for offspring sometimes causes them to come out of the Untersberg and appropriate to themselves children of men, such as they find lost or astray within their realm. For this reason they are called "wild," although I wish to gracious that I would never meet with anything less wild than they. I always found them very lovely, and I now understand the meaning of those popular tales which speak of children of peasants that have been abducted by these spirits, and taken into the Untersberg, where they lived among the "wild women," who treated them kindly, and played with them; and after a certain time sent them back to their parents loaded with gifts.

The comet-drivers

VI
LUCIFER

THE TEMPLE OF LUCIFER

ADALGA, like all the rest of the gnomes, was a spirit, in the same sense as we are spirits ourselves; the term "spirit" implying a centre of consciousness or intelligence, irrespective as to whether the form in which that spiritual power or energy dwells is visible to somebody or everybody or nobody. In this sense the essence of everything is spirit, and every living form is a dwelling-place or vehicle for a conscious spiritual energy, be it latent or active, as it could not otherwise be, if the world, as demonstrated by our best philosophers, is, with all its seen and unseen forms, nothing else but a manifestation of All-consciousness, an attribute of the Divine Mind.

In taking this view I am well aware that I am assuming an attitude directly opposed to that of Professor Thomas Cracker, in his capacity as a representative of that modern science which regards the universe as being made up of dead lumps of matter, in which, in some inexplicable way, life and consciousness are produced by means of mechanical motion, due to the friction caused by their coming accidentally in contact with each other. I am also clairvoyant enough to foresee that Mr Cracker and his learned colleagues will treat this story with contempt, if they should ever condescend to notice it; but this cannot be helped, and I resign myself to my fate.

I will therefore not enter into a discussion concerning the merits of a philosophy resulting from looking at the universe in its spiritual aspect, or compare it with the absurdities resulting from a blind belief in materialism and its superstitions, but proceed to say that Adalga being a spirit, in possession of an intelligence not due to mechanical friction, but due to the presence of an intelligent power in her own constitution, this intelligence of which she was possessed became manifested in her, and as time went on its manifestations increased, as might have been scientifically proved by the observation that she became more clever and intelligent. From this it may be inferred that the princess was in possession of a mind capable of cognizing things by means of her bodily senses, and the facts which I witnessed every day went to corroborate the correctness of this theory. Moreover, there were indications that her mind was capable of cognizing the actuality of spiritual truths or principles; but being only a gnome, she was not capable of intricate reasoning and complicated argumentation.

I often argued with her about the supposed immortality of the soul, and it seemed to me that Adalga was not substantial enough to be more than an ideal, and could therefore not be an enduring reality, because ideals require substance for becoming realised. In other words, the princess often appeared to me like a thought, that may delight the present generation but be forgotten by the next. What she needed was "matter" or firmness, such as results from fixedness or stability of the spirit, and I came to the conclusion that I could supply her with the required material elements by her union with me. I know that I will be accused of making wild statements, unsupported by any well-authenticated scientific theory, but it will be seen that by means of my logical and inductive reasoning I arrived at the end at the same result, which Adalga seems to have perceived instinctively, and without any scientific training of

 The comet-drivers

her imagination, merely by her own direct perception.

It may be inferred that Adalga had a soul, because she was alive and capable of having emotions, and in that soul seemed to be dormant a spark of a higher or spiritual life or consciousness, producing in her longings for the unknown, such as were expressed in her song in the cave; longings which she herself could not explain, be it that her mind was not sufficiently developed to understand her own nature, or that she was deficient in a scientific training of her imagination.

The tribe to which Adalga belonged was that of the Sagani, the noblest of all the tribes among the gnomes, whose intellectual capacity was nearest to that of man. Being a Sagana, it was in her power to elongate her body, a circumstance which was at first terrifying, and afterwards somewhat annoying to me; for often while we were sitting side by side, with arms interlinked, and engaged in the sweet occupation of exchanging our sentiments, would she forget herself, and suddenly elongating her body shoot up some twenty-five feet high by sheer force of habit, upsetting me or carrying me up into space before I had time to let go of her arm or take it away from my waist. I begged her to restrain herself, and not to do so again in my presence; but self-restraint is a power entirely unknown among the gnomes. It is only possible for those beings who are in possession of a certain amount of spiritual self-consciousness, or, in other words, who feel or know that they are somehow superior to their own nature, as I am bound to say, even if I risk being accused of believing in the existence of something supernatural. The gnomes do not realise anything higher than their own elemental nature, and can therefore not restrain it. Only man can do or keep from doing certain things from a sense of duty and superiority. It is true that even animals seem to restrain themselves, but it is their fear or other instincts which restrains them, and not the experience of anything higher than their natural animal state; they do not experience any superiority over their animal nature, because no such superiority is existing in them; their motives for action are all to be found in their own natural world, while man's motives may sometimes spring from something superior than his own animal nature, namely, from a higher and divine nature in him.

To my remonstrances the princess used to answer:

"It is my longing for the high, the sublime, and exalted which causes me to elongate my body involuntarily. I wish to grasp the infinite, and this makes me shoot up involuntarily."

"This, my dear," I replied, "is not the proper way, and would not be permitted in polite society among us. Moreover, you cannot reach infinitude in this manner, which reminds me of the performances of certain scientific theologians, who continually keep searching for God by means of a telescope. We cannot reach the infinite by stretching our limbs; we must grow and unfold from within by the power which we accumulate. This power, as it grows and expands, will cause our souls to unfold and develop. Instead of seeking for support outside of ourselves, we ought to be like a storage-battery, filled with a living power, that will radiate all over the world. This power is called love."

"And can your clever men of science make love?" asked the princess.

"Oh yes!" I answered; "love-making is a favourite occupation with many of our people; but the love they make is not the genuine article, but merely a spurious imitation. Genuine love cannot be made or manufactured, it is eternal; all we can do is to establish the conditions under which it may become manifest."

"Oh how I wish I could learn all that you know!" exclaimed Adalga. "Will you not instruct me?"

"With the greatest pleasure!" I answered. "The first thing which you will require to learn is to distinguish the true from the false. You gnomes know that which is true, because you perceive it, but you do not distinguish it sufficiently from that which is false, because falsehood is unknown to you. The first requirement for you to attain a higher state of civilisation is therefore to become acquainted with all sorts of falsehoods, deceptions, and lies."

Adalga seemed to be frightened, and I therefore continued to explain.

"Listen!" I said. "You know that which is, because you perceive it; but you must also learn to know that which is not, so that you may distinguish it from that which actually is, and not mistake mere appearances for realities."

"But if that which is not has no existence, how can we know it?" asked the princess.

"We cannot truly know that which is not," I said, "except by experiencing its nothingness. We must ourselves become liars and cheats, otherwise we will always have only a vague idea of what lying and cheating means. We must be able to perceive that which is not, so that we may get some idea of that which is."

"But how can I perceive that which is not," asked Adalga, "if there is nothing to perceive?"

"In the easiest way in the world," was my answer. "It only requires a scientifically trained imagination. We will then be able to see anything we like, even if there is nothing."

The princess was delighted. She looked at me with a face expressive of great admiration, and said:

"As the glowing tiny spark of the ruby grows into a large red light when it is joined by the flame, so my admiration of thee grows in beholding thy knowledge. No longer art thou veiled to my eyes, for the secret has been revealed, and I behold in thee not a man, but one of the sons of Lucifer, the god to whom no gnome can approach."

"Nonsense!" I said. "The story of Lucifer is only a nursery

tale, an exploded humbug, annihilated by science. What do you mean? Who is the Lucifer of whom you are speaking?"

"The god of darkness! He who knows that which is not and does not know that which is; he whose temple is beyond the limits of our city, whose portals no gnome can enter without losing his light. Follow me!"

Thus saying, the princess dissolved, and assuming her spherical shape floated away, while I followed her as fast as my legs would carry me, for my curiosity was greatly excited.

Beyond the city of Gnana, the capital of the kingdom of the gnomes, there is a wilderness composed of forests, jungles, and swamps. There you find sandy deserts interspersed with an occasional spot of verdure, and innumerable bogs over which will-o'-the-wisps are aimlessly wandering. Some parts are entirely bare of vegetation, others are covered with a luxuriant growth of curious trees, resembling the Poison Ivy (Atrus toxicodendron), upon which grows a tasteless fruit. There was also a species of crab-apple trees, and another bearing a certain kind of nuts, which were awfully hard to crack, and contained nothing but ashes. In some places the spot was covered with fine-looking but poisonous toad-stools, and the ways were full of entangled vines and briers. The main road was leading to nowhere; for after following it until you were exhausted to death, you would find yourself exactly upon the spot from which you started at the beginning.

In the midst of this labyrinth there stands a curious-looking castle, looking very solid and strong, with many fortifications; built of sandstone. There are thick walls, surrounded by moats, buttresses, and counterforts guarded by banquettes, abuttes, scarps and palisades, fraises and parapets, ditches and trous de loup, all of which look very formidable; but the light has such a peculiar influence upon the material of which the castle is built, as to cause the walls to decompose and rapidly crumble away. The very foundation of the building has so little solidity

　　　The comet-drivers

as to cause the walls slowly but continually to sink, so that it requires a continual repairing and building at the top to cause the castle to remain above the ground and to maintain a respectable appearance.

It was in front of that castle that the princess reassumed her corporeal form, and as I approached nearer I found the walls ornamented with skeletons and skulls, and upon the top of the building waved a flag, consisting of a great many pieces of cloth of many different sizes and colours, sewed together in a haphazard manner, and this flag bore the inscription:

Knowledge is Power.

At the entrance of the fort there was a kind of a temple made of jet-black stone. A few steps led up to a door.

"These walls," said my companion, "are the remnant of what was once a city built by a now extinct race of demons," and pointing to the temple, she added, "Here is the temple of him who knows that which is not, and does not know that which is."

"And what is to be seen in there?" I asked.

"Who knows?" exclaimed the princess. "This place is shunned by every gnome, and no one dares to enter. It is said, however, that it is inhabited by insane spooks, and by the remnant of a certain class of people who have spent their lives in doing many useless things. They are said to follow their accustomed occupations in an automatic manner, doing the same things over and over again without coming to an end."

"And who were they, when they lived?" I asked.

"Nobody knows," answered Adalga. "None of these creatures knew himself while he lived; how could anybody know him after he died?"

I expressed my determination to enter, upon which the princess grew very much alarmed, and begged me to desist; but the more she sought to dissuade me from my purpose, the greater grew my curiosity to investigate the mysteries of Lucifer's temple.

"Do not enter, O Mulligan!" cried the princess. "It will destroy your light."

"I have no light to lose," I answered. "I am not a gnome."

"Woe to me!" she cried. "Shall I lose you and my life even before our union has become completed! Stop this rash undertaking! Stop, O Mulligan, stop!"

"I must see the mystery of Lucifer!" I exclaimed, while tearing myself away from Adalga's arms and making a rush for the door, which I entered, while the princess remained outside, wringing her hands and filling the kingdom of the gnomes with her lamentations and cries.

The room into which I entered appeared at first perfectly empty and dark; but after a little while I was able to see two luminous spots of a reddish yellow light at a distance, and some dark and voluminous object loomed up. Vague and undefinable nebulous shapes seemed to be flitting before my eyes and moving about. I confess that at first I experienced a feeling of something like fear and repugnancy; but nerving my courage, I went forward, and soon stood before a gigantic figure representing a green frog squatting upon a stone, and from the eyes of the frog shone the phosphorescent lights which I had observed when I entered, looking like two fiery balls. The jaws of the frog were wide open, as if it were ready to devour anything whatever coming within its reach. Gradually my eyes became accustomed to the gloom, and I could read an inscription upon the pedestal saying—

Nulla Ratio Sine Phosphore.

Many years after that event I presented this inscription to the Academy, and respectfully asked for an explanation of its meaning. There were a few who claimed that it said it was necessary for the brain to contain phosphorus, so that the principle of mind could become active therein, and make

     The comet-drivers

a man capable of reasoning; but the great majority of the Academicians claimed that reason itself was a product of phosphorus, and a mode of motion of its molecules in the brain.

I was no longer afraid. I climbed upon the pedestal and examined the head of the frog, when I found that in the place of a brain there was a large lump of phosphorus enclosed in a film of coloured glass. It was the light of the phosphorus shining through the coloured glass that caused the lurid glow which came from the goggle eyes of the frog.

This discovery made me laugh. "This, then," I said to myself, "is the celebrated Lucifer of whom the gnomes are afraid. Evidently the scientists of that extinct race attempted to create a living and thinking being in an artificial manner by making a compound of phosphorus to serve for a brain; but for all that they produced nothing but the dead image of a bull-frog." I felt tempted to smash the frog or to take the phosphorus, but for some cause, which is not quite clear to myself, I made up my mind to let it alone.

I now became also able to see more clearly the nebulous forms that wandered about in space, and to my horror I found among them not only the shades of some prominent people well known in history, but also the apparitions of some persons with whom I was well acquainted. Among them was one who had spent all his life in trying to invent a perpetuum mobile, and who to my knowledge is still living. As I approached him, I found him engaged in his usual occupation. He seemed to be aware of my presence, for he said—

"There is only one little hinge which prevents the instrument from going. When this is overcome it will work all right, and my name will be inscribed in the register of the Academy."

"And of what benefit," I asked, "will it be to you to have your name thus inscribed, when you yourself are only a ghost?"

It is said that ghosts, like the gnomes, cannot speak otherwise than as they think, because they have not sense enough to prevaricate. He looked at me in surprise, and merely answered—

"Fool!"

He had become so much emaciated, and his voice sounded so hollow, that I began to doubt whether he actually was the one I had known in our world; I therefore asked him who he was.

"Alas!" replied the ghost mournfully, "I do not know who I am. While I was among the living I knew everything about science and philosophy, medicine and theology, spiritism and psychic research, but unfortunately I never knew myself. It is said that I made many inventions and discoveries, but as I do not know myself, I do not know who invented and discovered these things, and whether it was I or another; moreover I have forgotten them all."

"But," I said, "why do you not try to find out who you are?"

Another deep sigh expressed the profundity of his grief as he said—

"Life is short, and I have no time to attend to that matter. First, I will finish this perpetuum mobile, and after that I may have leisure to find out who I am and for what purpose I exist. I have now put these wheels together for the ten thousand six hundred and ninety-fifth time, and there is only one little hinge. After this business has been accomplished I will turn my attention to more serious matters."

I felt a deep pity for the ghost, in whom I now well recognised my friend, for the words spoken by him I had often heard him express before. I therefore said—

"There is nothing to be said against entering into scientific experiments and increasing one's store of knowledge in regard to the laws of external nature and its phenomena; but a far more important thing it is to know one's own self and the object of one's existence, so that one may act accordingly, and make the best use of life."

"I know it," answered the ghost, "and I often said so myself, but I have now no time to attend to philosophical questions; I must finish this wheel."

"Perhaps," I said, "you would succeed better if you were first to learn to know your real self and its powers, and construct your wheel afterwards, if you should still think it worth the while to spend your time with such nonsense."

When I said this the ghost became very angry, and said—

"Avaunt, fool! and do not torment me. Get thee gone!"

So saying, the ghost snapped his jaws at me in a furious manner, and I barely escaped having my ear bitten off.

I mournfully turned away, sadly grieved that such a bright intellect should have been allowed to evaporate in dreams; but I knew that it was of no use to argue with him, for my own experience with the jumping-jack had taught me what a great power a fixed idea has over the mind.

Another ghost, fearfully emaciated, now attracted my attention. He looked more like the shadow of a skeleton than a man, and was evidently at the point of starvation, but engaged in the ludicrous occupation of composing a bill of fare, while he himself had nothing whatever to eat. I looked over his shoulder and saw him write out the following prescription:

Dejeuner à la fourchette.

Huîtres.

Consommé tapioca à la Julienne. Potage crême d'asperges.

Fruites au bleu; sauce à la Russe.

Bœuf à la mode aux maccaroni a l'Italienne.

Selle de mouton Hollandaise.

Œufs bruillé aux melettes.

Emincé de faiseur à la Windsor.

Canard braisé en Bordeaux.

Omelette souflée. Plum pudding.

Purée de pommes et nocles au naturel.

Fromage suisse. Glacé panachée aux gaufres cornets.

Bordeaux. Champagne.

Desert. Café.

"And where are all the good things whose names you have written?" I asked.

"This," he answered haughtily, "you will have to find out yourself. It is sufficient if I indicate to you the order in which I might eat them if I had them. Does this not satisfy you?"

"It might satisfy my curiosity," I replied, "but it will not cure your hunger or make you fat. You seem to me to need something more substantial than mere theories."

"Knowledge is power!" said the ghost. "When you have acquired the knowledge how to eat in good style you may apply it as soon as you get the chance."

"Look here, my friend," I answered, "it seems to me that you need very much a chance to get something to eat, even if it were not served up in the style proposed by you. Would it not be better to let this bill of fare alone, and seek for some food?"

"I have no time to attend to that," replied the ghost. "I must first settle the theory; the practice may wait."

"But by that time," I said, "you may be starved to death."

This remark seemed to annoy the ghost, for it was true, and ghosts never like to hear any truth that goes against their own pet theories. Being themselves made up of delusions, a spark of truth is to them a foreign element, and burns them like fire.

"Go away!" he cried angrily. "Do not waste my time. I shall not permit any scoffing at science."

As I turned away I saw another ghost of still more pitiful

aspect, clothed in rags, the very personification of abject poverty. Want and misery were looking out of his hollow cheeks, and his eyes were buried deep in their sockets. He was making a long calculation.

"What are you calculating?" I asked.

"Do not disturb me," he said. "I am calculating the interest which I would receive if I were to inherit all of Mr Vanderbilt's money and estates, and how much, with the compound interest added to it, it would amount to in one hundred years, and I want to see whether this would be enough to enable me to live comfortably in my old age. I have now been over this calculation for many years, but I must begin it again, because the value of the stocks has again changed, and there is a difference in the amount of the interest."

I was surprised to hear that a person of such a beggarly appearance should have such excellent financial prospects, and I said:

"When do you expect to make that inheritance, and could you not get now some money on credit on the strength of your prospective income?"

To this the ghost replied:

"Alas, no! I have no prospect of making any inheritance whatever, and there is no one who would lend me a penny; but it is such a comfort to know how much money I might enjoy if I had it, and what an amount of interest the capital would bring if I were in possession of it."

"And could you not do some work for the purpose of earning some money?"

"Alas, no! I have no time for that; I must finish this calculation first."

"But what good will it do to you," I asked, "to know all that stuff, as long as you are in such a state of poverty?"

The ghost shivered. He looked at me scornfully, and said

in an angry tone—

"Knowledge is power! Do not waste my precious time. Begone!"

Thus going from one to another, I found all these spectres employed in occupations which had no practical purpose, and served at best to amuse their imagination or gratify their curiosity. They all spent what little energy was left in them for the purpose of wasting their time, making themselves believe that they were doing something useful. They were all occupied with that which is not, and did not know that which is. They amused themselves, so to say, in worrying about the question what nothing might be if it were something, and in doing so they turned the only something they had, namely, their energy, into nothing. They were all dreams themselves, products of dreams, existing in dreams, leading a dream-life and doing nothing but dreaming; all they did was imaginary and had its origin in their own imagination. One of the ghosts, becoming angry, flew at me and stumbled and fell down. Thereupon it never occurred to him that he could get up again, but he remained floundering upon the floor, uttering pitiful lamentations. Some ghosts were playing cards, and although their continual losing was a source of annoyance to them, they had not the power to stop; others imagined that they had to imitate everything that they saw another ghost doing. This class was very large. One ghost practised target-shooting, but as he was all the time looking in quite another direction than where the target was, he always missed the mark; but wept bitterly and complained of his want of luck. But it is not possible to mention all the follies which I saw the ghosts commit in the palace of Lucifer; they were like insane people, reasoning cleverly but without being in possession of reason. I pitied them, and sick at heart I turned towards the door.

In the meantime, owing to the cries of distress uttered by the princess, great crowds of gnomes had gathered in front of the temple, but none dared to enter. The king and the queen and all the court had arrived. They were all running and floating to and fro and talking and gesticulating, everybody giving some good advice which nobody followed; they did not know what to do. That anyone could enter Lucifer's temple and come out again alive, or otherwise than blind or insane, seemed to them an impossibility. The king looked very grave and the princess was in despair.

"After all," I heard the queen say to the princess, while trying to comfort her, "Mulligan is nothing but a hobgoblin."

"No!" cried Adalga, "I know he is a man!"

While speaking these words the princess elongated her body to its full length, and looking towards the temple, saw me standing upon the threshold, and in spite of the cries of her mother, who tried to stop her, she flew to me and the next instant she was in my arms. The door had not yet been closed, and from the interior a ray of yellowish light, coming from the eyes of the green frog, fell upon the princess. I sought to shield her with my person, but it was already too late, for that ray mingling with the blue in Adalga's sphere, immediately produced therein a permanent shade of green.

A shout of joy arose from the multitude when they saw me issue from the temple, and never-ending hurrahs resounded; but this was changed to groans of distress when they beheld the change of colour which had taken place in the princess. The king was very much distressed, and while pulling his hair and beating his sides, he cried:

"Unfortunate was the hour when this magician entered my kingdom. Was it not enough that our beloved daughter had the misfortune of falling in love with this wretch and taint her beautiful silver white with a nasty blue? Having given her the blues, he now causes her to expose herself to the rays of the frog. Oh that I had never been born, or seen the hour of such misery! Let the executioner come immediately and execute the sentence of death."

A storm of indignation arose, and the vivisectors appeared. However, I was not afraid; I knew now the character of the gnomes and knew what to say.

"May it please your majesty," I said, "as well as our gracious queen and all the venerated assembly, to behold their beloved princess in this beautiful garment of green, whose splendour surpasses everything that has ever been seen before or may be seen afterwards. I call those present to witness that the princess never was so charming as since she has turned green. Green is the colour of hope, and indicates the beginning of wisdom. In the kingdom of man green is the favourite colour. Green is the grass of the earth, the trees and plants, and even the ocean waves turn green when they come kissing the shore. But why should I waste words in praising a colour whose superiority is acknowledged by everyone who is capable of judging its beauty? Has not her gracious majesty, the queen herself, shown the superiority of her taste by choosing the emerald as the jewel of her heart, and adorning her person with green as the true expression of her excellent qualities? Verily, I am giving only expression to the feeling of every intelligent gnome who loves his dynasty and his country, if I request you to join me in the cry—'Hurrah for green!'"

And "Hurrah for green!" was shouted by all, over and over again. Owing to my eloquent speech green at once became the fashionable colour, and everyone wanted to become green. They lauded and praised me as the benefactor of gnomekind, and the ladies thronged around me, congratulating me, and begging of me to give them a shade of green. When order was somewhat restored I made a few more remarks, calling everyone a traitor who would not join me in my predilection for green. I said that the princess and I loved each other, and that I would have married her in spite of her being blue; but now, as she had turned green and resembled her mother, she

     The comet-drivers

had become a thousand times dearer to my heart.

Here, however, I am bound to confess for the sake of truth that my statements were not strictly correct, for the queen's colour was of the pure and beautiful hue of the emerald, while the colour of the princess was an impure or dirty green, not at all comparable with the former. However, we all knew that on certain occasions a few little rhetorical liberties must be permitted.

The king was very much pleased; he believed every word I said. He called me his benefactor and saviour of his country. He conferred on me on the spot the office of Grand Chancellor of the Kingdom and Superintendent of Public Schools. He decorated me with the insignia of the Order of the Bull-frog, and consented that the ceremony confirming my engagement to the princess should take place immediately, to be followed by the marriage as soon as the three dwarfs would return with their discovery of the sun.

When the king had finished giving this decision, he embraced me and the princess, and this was also done by the queen and her maids, by the ministers and high dignitaries that were present, and by their wives and daughters, mothers and mothers-in-law; but the rest of the gnomes danced and shouted and stood upon their heads, swinging their legs as a token of joy. The princess was radiant with smiles, and we all were very happy. Cravatu even said that this was the happiest day that had ever been seen in the kingdom.

We returned to the palace, where preparations were made immediately for a great festival. The best mushrooms that could be found were collected and prepared by the best cooks. Some were boiled, others stewed, and some dished up raw. The queen herself assisted in the kitchen work. The court musicians arrived, the palace was decorated in great style, and deputations came, not only from all parts of Bimbam's country, but also from neighbouring states. I received a fine suite of apartments adjoining those of the king and the princess, together with a lot of attending servants to keep my rooms continually illumined, for which purpose the most radiant gnomes were selected.

But I will not impose upon the patience of the reader by describing the festivities which took place when the still beautiful princess Adalga became Mr Mulligan's bride. I will only say that during the most solemn moment of the ceremony, when the mutual promises were exchanged, it seemed to me that I distinctly heard the triumphant croaking of a frog; but no one else noticed it, and it may have been only an effect of my own imagination.

VII
DIGGING FOR LIGHT

EDUCATING THE GNOMES

I WAS now tolerably well satisfied. From the abject state of a nobody, existing only as a "subject" for scientific observation, looked upon as a hobgoblin, and doomed to vivisection prisoner of a jumping-jack, I had suddenly become somebody of importance, owing to my cleverness and to the credulity of the king. I saw myself now raised to the highest dignity in the kingdom of the gnomes, and engaged to a most amiable and charming—even if a little green—princess, and there was momentarily nothing to be desired except the discovery of the sun and the completion of my marriage.

This discovery of the sun caused me a certain uneasiness; but I hoped that the king would not continue to insist upon that condition. A considerable time had elapsed, and nothing was heard of the dwarfs or their expedition. It seemed to me not at all improbable that they had fallen into the hands of Professor Cracker, and were now bottled up in alcohol, adorning the shelves of some museum. At all events, I had not the faintest hope that even if they were to return, they would have discovered anything worth speaking of, or be able to describe it, and I therefore thought of means for persuading the king to alter the stipulation in regard to my marriage, and to permit it to take place before the discovery of the sun. This I did not think very difficult, for the king was very changeable and did not seem to know his own mind. Although, whenever he got some idea into his head, he was very stubborn and self-willed, nevertheless he was easily led by the nose by those who knew how to flatter him. His capriciousness was shown by the rashness with which he ordered my execution, and his instability by changing his mind and making me Grand Chancellor of his kingdom.

For this purpose I sought and obtained an interview with the king, and asked his consent that the marriage between myself and the princess should not be delayed. I proved to him by arguments that the sun could not do otherwise but exist, and that it was merely a question of time to discover it; that this event would perhaps not take place as soon as we wished it, but that this would make no difference to the sun. I took especial pains to explain to him that the interests of the state would suffer by my being doomed to live as a bachelor.

But the king had never studied logic, and was inaccessible to my arguments.

"I want the sun!" he cried, growing more than usually red in his face.

To this I replied—

"If your majesty will permit, we all know that life, and light, and heat come from the sun. The sunlight does not penetrate into your kingdom because the rays of the sun are refracted upon the surface of the earth; but the caloric rays of the sun penetrate through these rocks, otherwise there would be no heat and life, and everything would be cold and dead in this place. Now, as you feel the warmth within your residence, you will easily see that there must be a sun."

"I see nothing," answered the king. "All that you say may be as you say, but it does not enable me to perceive the sun."

"And would it not be just as well," I said, "if your majesty

          The comet-drivers

would accept my information that there is a sun? If I tell you so, you will know it, and knowledge is power."

But the king would not agree. "I perceive," he said, "that you tell me that there is a sun; but for all that I do not perceive the sun itself, and cannot eat it or have it deposited in my treasury."

This stubbornness of Bimbam I. irritated me somewhat, and I said—

"All that your majesty says goes to show that the gnomes will have to travel still a long way before they will come up to our standard of science. We, the scientists of the human kingdom, do not need to acquire or possess or even to see anything, much less to eat or absorb it into our own constitution; it is quite sufficient for us to have a theory about it which is believed to be correct. This is what we consider to be real knowledge."

"What a fools' paradise this must be," exclaimed the king. "In our country we enjoy that which we are and possess, and care very little about theories and opinions."

While we were engaged in this conversation Cravatu entered, and brought the news that the three dwarfs had returned, and that everything had come out exactly as I predicted; for these imbeciles, not having sense enough to find their way back, had been found in the vicinity of the place where they had been left. All that could be made out by their incoherent speech was that they had seen something, but what that was nobody knew, for they were totally unable to describe it.

This fulfilment of my prediction raised me still higher in the estimation of the king, who, seeing that I could foretell future events, looked upon me as a kind of supernatural being, and wanted to be instructed in that art.

"It is very easy," I answered. "If your majesty will only study logic, and, instead of directly looking at a thing, reject the evidence of your senses and begin to argue from the basis of what you assume to be true. Logic is the method of reasoning from particulars to generals, or the inferring of one general proposition from one or several particular ones; which means that instead of looking at a thing as a whole, and afterwards examining its parts and the relations in which they stand to it, we must look at some separate part and imagine the rest. It is a process of demonstrating to our own satisfaction and to the satisfaction of everyone who believes in our judgment——"

Here I was interrupted by the loud snoring of the king who had gone to sleep in his chair. The sudden stopping of my speech had the effect of awakening him. He yawned, and elongating his body to its full length, he stretched his limbs, and then went on to say—

"This is very interesting, and I want to have this method introduced in all the schools of my kingdom; but for the present the most important thing is the discovery of the sun, and I want you to discover it without further delay."

I suggested that this might be done after my wedding; but the king sternly replied, "No sun, no marriage! That's all."

Being so near to the completion of my happiness, I was exceedingly grieved to see my hopes wrecked by their fulfilment being made to depend upon an impossible condition; but a happy thought struck me, and I said—

"I assure your majesty that the sun is right over our heads, and there is nothing to prevent you from seeing it as soon as you will get out of this mountain, except the atmospheric air, which, unfortunately enough, is impenetrable to your sight, while I can easily enough see through it. Under these circumstances, the only thing that can possibly be done will be to cut a hole through the air, and make a tunnel deep enough until you will reach the outer limits of the atmosphere, when there will be nothing to prevent you from seeing the sun."

This proposal pleased the king exceedingly, and Cravatu

                 The comet-drivers

could find no words strong enough to express his admiration of my wisdom. They both knew already enough of logic to understand that they would be able to see the sun if there were nothing to hinder them from seeing him. Accordingly orders were immediately issued that the best labourers, miners, and mechanics should be selected for the purpose of cutting a hole in what they called the "sky," for the sky for them began there where their own element, the earth, ended.

On the very next day the work was begun. They selected a place on the very top of the Untersberg. The Pigmies drilled the holes, the Vulcani did the blasting, the Cubitali furnished the required materials, and the Sagani superintended the work, giving directions. We had the pleasure of seeing that already during the first twenty-four hours a hole of about ten feet depth and with a diameter of ten feet was made as the beginning of the tunnel for enlightenment.

Thus day by day, or, to speak more correctly, night after night, the work went on; for when it is day in our world no work is done by the gnomes, as with the beginning of sunrise they fall into a state of lethargy, from which they awaken only after the night has set in. Every night the king and the queen with her maids, the princess, myself, and the high dignitaries of the kingdom, went out to see the progress made in the work of the tunnel, and every night the hole grew deeper to a certain extent, according to the quality of the material which had to be cut; but when it began to dawn upon the surface of the earth the gnomes went to sleep and slept so well that nothing could have awakened them from their slumber.

In the meantime I considered it my duty to give great attention to the education of the gnomes, and to the development of their power of drawing inferences from things unknown. For the purpose of enabling them to distinguish the true from the false, I established schools of logic all over the country, in which all sorts of lies were taught, so as to give them a chance for using their own common sense and finding out the truth for themselves by overcoming the falsehood. Soon I was in possession of a corps of capable liars for assisting me in this work; but the education of the princess I took into my own charge.

At first Adalga did not enjoy the lessons, which is only natural, as the birth and beginning of everything is painful and difficult, but after a while she became delighted with my instructions. As my method may prove to be interesting and instructive to my compatriots engaged in pedagogical enterprises, I will illustrate it by an example.

First of all I tried to explain to the princess, by practical experiment, that a good scientist can never know anything whatever; he can only know what a thing is not, but not what it is, and from what he perceives that it is not he draws his inferences as to what it may be.

Thus, for instance, taking a stone and handing it to Adalga, I said—

"Queen of my heart! will you tell me what this is?"

"With pleasure!" she answered. "It is a stone."

"How do you know it?"

"Because I see it."

"Sight is deceptive," I said. "It may be a pumpkin."

"I do not care what it may be; I know it is a stone."

"How can you prove it?"

"I do not need to prove it. I know it, and so does everybody who knows a stone."

"You cannot know it," I said, "unless you can give any rational reason for your belief."

"I do not need to give any reasons for it. I am satisfied to know what I know."

I saw that I could not get the better of her in this way, so

I said—

"Will you have the kindness to imagine this stone to be a pumpkin?"

"Well, Mr Mulligan!" she answered, "if this gives you pleasure, I shall imagine it to be a pumpkin."

"Now take a bite of it, my darling," I said.

"I can't, and you ought not to ask me anything so absurd."

"But why can't you?"

"Because it is too hard."

"Exactly!" I exclaimed. "And now as you have discovered that it is too hard for being a pumpkin, you have a scientific right to infer that it is not a pumpkin and may possibly be a stone; quod erat demonstrandum."

This way of making a simple thing very complicated, according to the strict rules of exact science, pleased the princess very much and amused her greatly. It now became necessary to show to her how we may arrive at a knowledge of universals by drawing logical inferences from particulars. For this purpose I told her that we must never trust to our reason, but only put faith into our method of reasoning. Pointing to the stocking which the princess was just knitting, I asked her what it was.

"A stocking," she said. "I thought you knew that much already."

"Who is going to wear it?"

"I."

"And what are you?"

"A princess of this kingdom."

"Do all the princesses of this kingdom wear stockings?"

"All those whom I know."

"Very well!" I replied. "The consequence is that all the people who wear stockings are princesses of the kingdom of the gnomes."

This seemed strange to Adalga, but she could not prove that it was not so, and I proceeded to explain to her that the power to draw logical inferences was the highest power which a scientist could possess, and that by means of logic almost anything could be proved, be it true or false. Thus I proved to her by way of an illustration, first, that white was black; secondly, that black was white; and thirdly, that there was no colour at all.

"White, my dear!" I said, "is, as everybody knows, no colour at all; for it is produced by a combination of all the prismatic colours in the same proportion as they exist in the solar ray, where each colour neutralises the other. Now, if there is no colour, there can be no light, and where no light exists everything is as black as night, and if everything is black, white must be black also, and consequently white is black."

"Very strange!" exclaimed Adalga.

"If white is black," I continued, "it follows that black is white, because if there is no difference between two things they must be identical. Moreover, everybody knows that black is no colour at all, but the negation of colour, and it follows that if a thing has no particular colour of any kind, it must necessarily be white."

"Incredible!" exclaimed the princess.

"There is nothing incredible about it," I said. "It is all very reasonable. Moreover, there is no such thing as a colour at all, for what we call by that name refers only to a certain sensation which is produced in our brains by means of certain vibrations transmitted through the retina and the optic nerve. If you look at any coloured thing in the dark you will find it to be without any colour at all. The sensations we receive are only due to certain vibrations of something unknown."

"What is a vibration?" asked Adalga.

     The comet-drivers

"Vibration," I said, "is nothing but a certain kind of motion, and as motion per se does not exist, vibration is nothing, while that unknown thing which moves must be everything. But the existence of that unknown thing is not admitted by science, and consequently science knows nothing of everything, and of everything nothing, just as you like; and you can make nothing out of everything, and everything out of nothing, at your own pleasure."

The princess was delighted to hear that she could now make everything out of nothing, although for the beginning it could be done only theoretically, and her repugnance to philosophical hair-splittings faded away. She continued her lessons with great diligence, and very soon I had the pleasure of seeing that she believed nothing and denied everything. A few weeks more, and I was highly gratified to find that she could no longer tell a mock-turtle from a tommy cat without entering into a long series of arguments for the purpose of proving which was which. Unfortunately, in proportion as she lost her power of perceiving the reality, while improving in the practice of logic, her own light grew more and more dim, her luminosity less, and the green colour in her sphere darker; but I considered this as a matter of only secondary importance; for it is said that beauty is a perishable thing, while wisdom remains.

Sometimes she was inclined to worry about the fading of her charms, but I reasoned her out of it, saying: "If everything is nothing, then, as a matter of course, beauty also is nothing, and it is not worth the while to worry about the loss of nothing."

"But," objected Adalga, "if beauty is nothing and nothing is everything, beauty is everything, and we must do all we can to preserve it."

"Beauty," I replied, "among our people is the outcome of fashion. If it were to become fashionable in our world to wear goitrès and hunchbacks, everybody would find it beautiful and adopt it at once; and even if he did not find it beautiful, he would pretend to find it so. Thus it often happens that everybody wears a most ridiculous article of dress, not because he thinks it beautiful, but because he thinks that others do so. In this way the people act foolish, and silently laugh at each other for being such fools."

"This I should think to be very immoral," objected Adalga.

"Human morality," I replied, "is also a matter of custom. What is considered very moral among one nation or class of people is considered immoral among others. Some, for instance, regard stealing as a disgrace, others as a proof of great ingenuity. But we will not enter into these social questions. We would never come to an end. What you need for the purpose of evoluting into a higher and nobler sort of a being is, first of all, the three steps, or mental operations, by which you will proceed from particulars to generals, and from generals to still higher generalities by means of rejections and conclusions, so as to arrive at those axioms and general laws, from which we may infer, by way of synthesis, other particulars unknown to us, and perhaps placed beyond the reach of direct examination."

"Oh my!" exclaimed the princess, and I saw that my explanation was not very clear to her; but this is excusable in a gnome, and I did not despair.

There is nothing more certain than that religious speculation without science leads to superstition; but it is also true that scientific speculation in regard to philosophical questions leads to blind materialism and insanity, if it is carried on without any religious basis, which means spiritual perception of truth. Adalga overdid the thing, because she was of an impulsive, fiery nature, and not used to self-restraint, and when I discovered the mistake it was too late to remedy it. I had taught her never to take anything for granted, and the end of it was that she doubted my words, disputed and

     The comet-drivers

denied everything, and always did the very contrary of what we expected her to do. It is said that a little learning is a dangerous thing, and I would add that the greater the learning the greater the folly, if at the foundation of all that imaginary knowledge there is no instinctive perception of truth, or what we call intuition.

The head of the princess became developed at the expense of her heart. The vital powers, which ought to have been distributed harmoniously through her system, went almost exclusively to furnish her intellect, and the consequence was that her head increased enormously in size, while her heart began to shrink. Her sight became dim, so that she could no longer distinguish right from wrong; her joyfulness left her; she became dissatisfied with herself and with everything; a continual scowl rested upon her face, and it was no pleasure to spend an hour in her company. Her former friends stampeded when they saw her approach.

I often tried to make her understand that at the basis of all creation there was an universal power, which has no name, but which men call God, and which those who reject that term, because they have formed a false conception of that which is beyond all human conception, might call by some other name, such as Love, Reason, All-consciousness, Divine Wisdom, etc., and that she might feel the manifestation of that power within her own soul, if she would only pay attention to it.

"Prove it," she cried. "Prove that I have a soul, or that anybody has such a thing, and which has never been discovered by science, neither in the pineal gland nor in the big toe. Show me that soul, and let me examine it, and I will bottle it up and preserve it in the museum."

"Soul means life," I replied. "How can you know that you have a life, except by the fact that you are living?"

"Fiddlesticks!" exclaimed the princess. "There is no such thing as life. What seems life to you is only a phenomenon produced by the mechanical action of brain molecules, the result of indigestion."

I was frightened to see the effects which my premature revelation of the mysteries of science had upon the princess. In vain I reminded her of the sentiments which she formerly used to have, and which were expressed in her song in the cave at the time of our first meeting. She called all these things "childish fancies," unworthy of the serious attention of science. Alas! her study of the phenomenal side of nature would not have been objectionable if only her spiritual culture had not suffered by that; but while her intellect grew strong by overfeeding, her soul became starved to death; neither would she listen to my admonitions; she could not realise the possession of anything higher than the ever-doubting intellect, and this was probably because she was only a gnome.

One day, when I actually thought her reason was entirely gone, I said to her—

"Adalga, dear, do you know me?"

"Don't dear me," was her answer. "How can you ask such a foolish question? I know that I have an image of somebody on my brain, and that its name is said to be Mulligan, but whether your qualities correspond to that image or not I have not yet discovered. For all I know, the Mulligan with whom I fancy myself to be acquainted may be only a product of my own imagination."

"It seems you love me no more?" I inquired despondently.

"What is love but an effect of the imagination?" she answered. "If I chose to fall in love with a pitchfork, and bestow my affection upon it, it will do me the same service as to love Mr Mulligan."

"I assure you," I said, "true love is an entirely different thing. That which you describe is only some kind of fancy."

"Prove it," she exclaimed, as usual; but alas! I could not

     The comet-drivers

prove to her that whose existence she could not experience.

To make the matter short, Adalga became so scientific as to lose all her loveliness of form and character, and became overbearing, ugly, conceited, and foolish, and the same was the case more or less with all the rest of the gnomes. The whole population became clever and cunning, but, at the same time, lying and hypocritical. Formerly they had been moved, as it were, only by one will, namely, the will of the king; now everybody wanted to rule everybody else, and nobody rule himself or be ruled by another. There was nothing but quarrels, disputes, dissensions, dissatisfaction, and selfishness; the gnomes lost their perception of truth and their light. The kingdom grew dark.

Formerly everything had been peaceful; but now it became necessary to employ force for the purpose of keeping order. Each gnome cared only for his or her own interests, and this caused fights. One of the first requirements was the establishment of a police. I soon found that the employees of the government, including the police, could not be relied upon. I therefore had to establish a corps of detectives, and employ for that purpose the greatest rascals, because it is known that "it requires a thief to catch a thief." These detectives had again to be watched by others, and from this ensued an universal espionage, which was intolerable. Moreover, everybody seeing himself continually watched, was thereby continually reminded that it was in his power to steal, and the end of it was that the people considered it to be a great and praiseworthy act if one succeeded in stealing without getting caught.

At the time of my arrival it was the custom of the gnomes to believe everything that anybody said, but now it became fashionable never to believe anything whatever. The consequence was that each believed the other a liar; each mistrusted the other; nobody spoke the truth, if it was not in his own interest to do so. Nothing could be accomplished without bribery; crimes became numerous, and it became necessary to establish jails all over the country.

There was one curious feature noticeable, especially among the Sagani, who now constituted the great autocratic body of scientists. The more learned they became the more narrow-sighted they grew. They lost the power to open their eyes, and decided upon every question according to hearsay and fancy. Their limbs became atrophied, and their heads swollen. Some became so big-headed and top-heavy that they often lost their balance and fell down. It was especially funny to see how they tumbled about whenever one forgot himself, and by force of habit elongated his body. Finally, narrow-sightedness became so universal that a gnome without spectacles was quite a curiosity, and it has been reported that even children with spectacles upon their noses were born; but of this I have no positive proof.

To my horror, the head of the princess grew larger and stronger every day, and two hard horn-like excrescences began to appear upon it at the place where the phrenological bump of love of approbation is located. At the same time she grew exceedingly stubborn and vain. She was continually surrounded by flatterers who imposed upon her credulity. She could bear no contradiction, and nevertheless craved for disputes for the purpose of showing off her great learning. She lost her former natural dignity and self-esteem, and in its place she acquired a great deal of false pride; but her love of approbation revolted against the idea that anybody might consider her vain, and for the purpose of avoiding such a suspicion she joined gnomes of doubtful character, and went into bad company.

Let me draw a veil over the history of these sad events. Even now, although having resumed my individuality as Mr Schneider, I can look back only with deep regret upon the change that overcame the charming princess Adalga, owing

     The comet-drivers

to the ill-timed instruction of Mr. Mulligan. As to her father, the king, instead of comprehending the sad state of affairs of his kingdom, he took a very superficial view of it. He was delighted with the intellectual progress of the princess, and with the advancement of culture among his subjects, and he overwhelmed me with tokens of favour, calling me a public benefactor for civilising the gnomes.

Bimbam I. did not care to enter himself into the study of logic and elocution, nevertheless he did not wish to be regarded as a fool. He therefore tried to give himself an appearance of being learned, and whenever his arguments failed, he became very irascible, and lost his temper. He was excitable, but too great a lover of comfort to remain long in an excited state, and for this reason he was easily pacified. Often he would get raving mad, bucking his head against the walls; but a moment afterwards he would go to smoke his pipe, as if nothing had happened.

More and more the influence of the green frog was felt spreading through the kingdom, and there were some who claimed to have seen him wandering about the streets, spreading poisonous saliva from his mouth, from which green and red-spotted toad-stools grew. The world of the gnomes became continually more unnatural and perverted; impudence assumed the place of heroism, sophistry the mask of wisdom, lecherousness passed for love, hypocrisy paraded the streets under the garb of holiness; those who succeeded in cheating all the rest were considered the most clever; the most avaricious gnomes were said to be the most prudent; he who made the greatest noise was thought to be the most learned of all. Nor were the ladies exempt from this general degradation, for they assumed the most ridiculous fashions, putting artificial bumps on their backs and wearing tremendous balloons in the place of sleeves; they lost their simplicity, were full of affectations and whims, and to do anything whatever in a plain and natural way was considered vulgar.

But what is the use of continuing to describe conditions which everyone knows who has visited the Untersberg within the last few years? It is sufficient to say that the country of the gnomes at that time resembled to a great extent the human-animal kingdom of our days, and I would have wished to leave it if I had not considered it my duty to remain for the purpose of trying to undo some of the mischief which had ignorantly been caused by my prematurely opening the door of the palace of Lucifer.

VIII
WAR

DARK and gloomy grew the kingdom of the gnomes in proportion as the light of each individual inhabitant decreased. Many who formerly were like luminous spheres, shedding radiant rays to a considerable distance, now became like dim will-o'-the-wisps, or merely phosphorescent dots or firebugs. As the general darkness increased, the glow that came from the eyes of the green frog in Lucifer's temple, whose doors were now continually open, became more visible, and at certain times the frog actually seemed to be alive.

The ghosts in the temple continued their accustomed occupations without making any progress whatever. The perpetuum mobile was always on the point of completion, but never completed; the bill of fare was continually altered, but there was nothing to eat; and the calculations made by the imaginary heir produced no interest. All the ghosts repeated the same follies again, which they had been in the habit of enacting before.

Meanwhile the work in the tunnel went on with great speed, and the hole in the sky grew deeper every night; but it was impossible to say how long it would take to finish it, as the depth of the atmosphere which had to be penetrated was not known. I estimated it to be about one thousand miles, and calculating the work at about five feet a night, I found that the tunnel would be finished in 2924 years, which was rather a long time to wait for the completion of my marriage.

Moreover, one very serious inconvenience made itself perceptible. The working men had become so big-headed as to render it impossible for more than three gnomes to work in the tunnel at the same time without bumping their heads together. This delayed the progress and caused fights, and the question of widening the tunnel had to be taken into consideration, which would necessarily cause a considerable expense.

Already the country was groaning under the heavy burden of an exorbitant taxation required for the heads of science, who did the hard work of thinking, for paying salaries to professors, policemen, pensioners, supporting prisoners and blind people, and especially for supplying with luxuries the royal family and their hangers-on. Especially the princess required a great deal of cash for her support. Her external appearance had become rather uncanny, and she therefore needed costly dresses and ornaments to hide her deformities. Her head, having grown to an enormous size, resembled the show-case of a jeweller's shop, being hung over with chains and jewels, while a crown, or to speak more correctly, a tube of gold, adorned her occiput for the purpose of hiding the two horn-like excrescences.

I was one day consulting the king, and tried to demonstrate to him the necessity of using some economy and curtailing his private expenses, as otherwise the whole country would be involved in financial ruin; but I found him quite unreasonable in that respect.

"I should like to know," he exclaimed, "what is the use of my being the king, if I cannot get all the money I want?"

"Everything," I said, "belongs to your majesty, but it will be to your own advantage to see that the resources of the country are not squandered, for, when the production ceases, there will be no more income."

"Well," said the king, "if the people refuse to pay, I can

     The comet-drivers

still depend upon my army, and we shall see."

Just at that moment we were interrupted by loud reports like explosions, following each other in rapid succession. This was followed by shouts and cries, and immediately afterwards Cravatu came rushing into the palace, and approaching the king, he said:

"May it please your majesty to take command of the army. The labourers making the hole in the sky have perforated the frontier of the kingdom of the spirits of the air, and the inhabitants offer resistance."

The king, having still a certain amount of perception of truth, did not get at all excited upon hearing this news, but lighting his pipe, he took a few whiffs, and said:

"What about it? I do not blame them; we can do nothing else but retire."

Just then the princess entered, and, hearing these words, she exclaimed:

"Rot! who ever heard of a king of the gnomes being afraid of the spirits of the air?"

"I never," replied the king.

"Well then," continued Adalga, "we must beat back the intruders, and force our way through their kingdom."

The king was easily influenced, especially when his ambition was touched. Therefore the words of the princess caused him to fly into a rage. First he grew red in the face, his features expanded from ear to ear like an india-rubber bag. Next, he jumped several feet from the ground and came down again with a thump. After that he threw his pipe upon the floor so that it broke, and stamped upon it with his foot. Finally, he lowered his head and butted it against Cravatu; and, after all this was done, he began to yell, crying at the top of his voice: "We must drive the rascals away! We must force a passage through them!"

A tumult was heard in the ante-room, and directly numerous gnomes rushed in. They were merchants and traders, and came to make offers for furnishing supplies for the army. They were under-bidding each other, each offering to the king a greater bribe for accepting his offer. The king accepted some of the bargains which seemed to afford to him the greatest profit for his private purse, and the goods were delivered. They consisted of barrels labelled "flour," and filled with sand, carloads of "leather shoes" made of paste-board, wooden hams, and cartridges filled with sawdust; also something that looked like a cannon, but it was made of wood and varnished, so as to give it the appearance of bronze.

We left the palace, and the blowing of horns indicated the locality of the combat. On the way we met a train of wounded gnomes, some exhibiting a pitiful aspect. All the wounded had terrible burns and scalds, and the limbs of some were torn away. One poor fellow had lost the whole of his lower jaw, which was dreadful to see, and he seemed to suffer great pain.

"Why do not these people assume their ethereal forms and thus get rid of their suffering bodies?" I asked the minister.

"This art," answered Cravatu, "is now becoming very difficult, and there are very few capable of exercising it, since we have become so substantial. Moreover, these people cannot do so at all; because it is necessary for that purpose that one should entirely forget his body, and how could we do that, if the sensation of pain or of pleasure keeps our attention fastened to it? For the purpose of throwing off the mask of personality and entering into the state of selflessness, an entire forgetfulness of self is required, such as is almost impossible to attain in our present state of civilisation."

The wounded we met became more numerous as we approached the battle-field, and here and there could be seen a corpse, stiff and stark, slowly but surely evaporating. When we arrived the explosions had already ceased, and Clavo, the

     The comet-drivers

general in command, approached upon a bicycle and made his report. From this it appeared that in trying to enlarge the tunnel, the labourers had entered into side-issues, and by blowing out a large block of air, made an opening into a foreign region of unknown extent, which was inhabited by a tribe of sylphs or fairies, unknown to science and not yet classified. These spirits had resented the intrusion, and prevented the approach of our soldiers by pouring upon them sheets of fluid lightning, with the most destructive effect, so that all resistance was rendered impossible, and they were forced to retreat after experiencing a considerable loss.

"There is nothing to be done," said the general, after finishing his account, "but to let these airy spirits alone and begin a new tunnel in some other place. They are not of an aggressive character, and will not molest us if we go away. We have, anyhow, no right to trespass upon their territory."

"This is exactly what I always said," the king replied; "what business have we to meddle with these good spirits? Let us go."

But the princess interfered.

"Rot!" she cried: "Good spirits, indeed! Let them be exterminated! Will your majesty let them deprive us of our glory? Their resistance is an insult to you!"

No words can express the pitch of rage to which these words aroused the king. Growing purple in the face and fairly screaming, he elongated himself to three times his natural size, and bumping his head against the wall, as was his habit whenever he fell into a passion, he cried:

"Let them be exterminated! Their resistance is an insult to me! Kill them! Cut off their heads!"

And falling down in an epileptic fit, owing to the excessiveness of his fury, he stamped with his feet, and kept on yelling, "Kill them! Cut off their heads!"

I thought that perhaps the matter might be settled in an amicable manner, and therefore I told the king that rashness was not always the best policy, and I asked for permission to send a messenger, under the protection of a flag of truce, to see whether or not a treaty could be made with the spirits of the upper world.

"This is exactly what I always said," replied the king. "Rashness is not always the best policy. We must send a messenger by all means."

Accordingly Cravatu and myself were appointed to that office, and we went.

The undertaking was not without danger, as the nature of the enemy and their habits of thought were not known, and it was not at all improbable that we should receive a shot of lightning at our approach. However, we arrived safely at the lower end of the tunnel, and, looking up, we saw a great number of blue lights moving above like a swarm of bees.

Cravatu, putting his hands to his mouth, shouted up through the hole:

"Peace be with you!"

We listened. The motion among the bees increased, and after a while we heard a very sweet music, as if of a silver harp and lute. This was followed by a roll of thunder and a flash of lightning, doing however no harm.

"What does this mean?" I asked Cravatu, and he replied:

"I perceive that these people speak a language different from our own. They are spirits of sound, and express their thoughts in music. What they mean to say is that they are peaceable, if we let them alone, but that they have the power to defend themselves if we trouble them."

"Prove it," I involuntarily exclaimed, for I had adopted instinctively the habit of the princess, who wanted proofs for everything.

     The comet-drivers

"It is not a matter for proving, but of understanding," answered Cravatu.

"But how are we going to reply?" I asked. "Where can we find a dictionary of music, and who is going to compose the music, or fiddle it to them?"

Upon this Cravatu said:

"The language of music used to be known to us as the music of nature. In olden times the gnomes could understand it and speak it, and required no dictionary for its interpretation, because their simple minds understood that simple language. But now we gnomes have become so learned and scientific, and our minds so complicated, that it is possible for hardly anyone to understand a simple thing, or to express himself in a simple manner. Fortunately, I still find some knowledge of music in my rapidly fading memory, but I cannot answer in music. However, I know the language of flowers, and this is also an universal and natural language, somewhat akin to music, and, if I am not mistaken, these spirits will understand it."

This ingenuity of Cravatu pleased me very much. He was in fact still sound at heart, one of the brightest of the gnomes, and in spite of the progress of civilisation, in the midst of which he moved, he had still a certain amount of perception of truth, although on that very account he was much exposed to the ridicule of the scientists and made a target for their wit, because they did not believe in such a thing as intuition, and said that nobody could know anything except by way of information, inference, and by a trained imagination.

Cravatu now called some of the Acthnici, who, by the mysterious power which they possess, can create visible objects out of the invisible images existing everywhere in the astral light, and ordered them to produce a White Rose. This they did, and caused it to float slowly up through the hole.

"What does this signify?" I asked, and Cravatu answered—

"The White Rose asks: 'May I approach you?'"

We waited awhile, when down through the tunnel floated an Euphorbia. We saw it plainly, and had ample time to examine it; but at the moment when it touched the earth it vanished. This flower Cravatu interpreted as being intended to say—

"Why do you persecute us?"

Up went a Heliotrope to tell them—

"My heart longs for you."

And the answer came back in the shape of a Belladonna, indicating—

"We do not credit the honesty of your intentions."

To this we replied by sending up a White Lily for the purpose of testifying to the purity of our affection, whereupon we received a Violet bidding us—

"Hope!"

Up again went a Daffodil, to ask them not to be so cruel as to let us pine away in hopeless misery, and we waited.

A consultation seemed to take place among the bees. A great number of small lights were seen to gather around a large blue light in the middle, and a melodious humming was heard. Directly a leaf of a Fern floated down, bringing the answer—

"I will meet you," and in return we sent up a Geranium to inform them that we were waiting.

Soon after that a clear and beautiful accord was heard, and something luminous floated down through the tunnel, which I could not describe otherwise than as being an oval-shaped radiance of an exquisite rose-coloured light, composed of living sound, and emitting harmonious accords, like an Æolian harp. When it issued from the mouth of the tunnel, I perceived within its sphere the ethereal shape of an Oleander blossom, in the midst of which appeared the childlike and smiling face of a most charming fairy. These were then the spirits of flowers.

     The comet-drivers

Cravatu presented the fairy with a Jessamine blossom as a token of friendship, and invited her to accompany us to the king.

An accord, indicating consent, was the answer, and we returned with the fairy in our midst.

"Bring the prisoner!" exclaimed Adalga, assuming an air of scientific arrogance, when she saw us approaching. This rudeness offended me, and I said:

"This is not a prisoner, princess, but an ambassador coming to us, upon our invitation, and under the flag of truce. It is a fairy of high descent, and the law of justice demands that she be treated respectfully."

"Prove it!" answered the princess angrily.

"Justice," I said, "is not a thing to be proved, but to be practised."

While I spoke, the Oleander blossom gave forth a sweet melody of harmonious sounds, but Adalga looked at the fairy with a wicked glance in her eye, and said:

"A curious specimen, which we must not let escape. It will be quite an ornament to our museum."

"It will be no such thing," I answered indignantly. "This noble fairy is under my protection, and I shall protect her."

But the princess retorted in a haughty manner:

"The interests of science are first of all to be taken into consideration. It may not be strictly correct, in a legal sense, to retain the prisoner, but the end justifies the means."

To this the king added:

"I always told you so; the end justifies the means."

Upon this Adalga made a vicious grab at the Oleander blossom, trying to capture it, but did not succeed; for the rose-coloured radiance at once became transformed into a column of red vapour, which whirled away, while from its interior came a discordant sound indicative of disappointment and sorrow.

The princess flew into a rage, and elongating her body to the full length, struck at the column of vapour, but only to fall upon her nose, for the red cloud had already passed beyond her reach. We followed the fairy, but could only see the rose-coloured light floating back into the tunnel, where it disappeared, and after a little while a mournful strain of music was heard. We sent up a variety of flowers with a hope of renewing the negotiations; but they were not accepted. We received nothing but a rain of ashes, indicating that all prospects for an amicable understanding were at an end.

This failure to catch the spirit of sound caused to the princess a great deal of vexation, and she blamed us for not having closed up the mouth of the tunnel to prevent the return of the fairy. To this I replied:

"There is a certain amount of honour even among thieves; but to a person absorbed by a greed for gratifying his scientific curiosity in regard to that which belongs to the higher life, nothing is inviolable or sacred, and nothing safe from his attempts to uselessly and foolishly cause its destruction. Too clumsy, stupid, and cowardly to try to rise up to a conception of high and exalted ideals, those would-be scientists and pseudo-philosophers would like to entice those ideals, allure them by false promises, and drag them down into the manure in which they themselves love to roll; but thanks to the laws of the eternal spirit in nature, true goodness cannot be approached by evil, wisdom is not comprehensible to the fool, and purity does not amalgamate with filth."

"Prove it!" she cried, probably more from force of habit than as a result of reflection; for some remnant of reason left in her mind seemed to make her feel the idiocy of her requests, and, changing the subject, she said:

"Who is it that has caused me to pry with curious eyes

The comet-drivers

behind the veil of the unknown, and to strive to outstrip my own natural growth. Who caused the loss of my light, my beauty and purity, destroyed my ideals, and made me a slave to doubt? Who, but you yourself, has caused me to treat reason with contempt, to become blind through vanity, and deformed by scepticism? Who, but you, has presented us with a knowledge of evil, which to overcome we have not become strong enough? Who, but you, took away our power, by causing us to expend it in channels that did not belong to our true nature? You caused us to lose our ethereal state, so that now we have to creep like worms upon the earth, instead of sailing like eagles through space on wings of freedom, as was the custom of our race before you arrived. Now the hellish work has begun and it shall be finished, let the cost be what it may. The end must be made to justify the means."

The determined and clear manner in which Adalga spoke pleased me very much; it proved to me that there was still a lingering spark of reason in her. It was as if the falling upon her nose had awakened her finer sensibilities, and I was about to enter into a discussion of philosophical questions with her; but she would not listen. Turning to the king, she requested him to declare war immediately to the superior kingdom, to force its doors open, and to select the best troops for making the assault.

"You are the ruler of the world," she said to the king. "You are great and wise. No one will dare to resist you."

"Of course," answered the king, being much tickled by her flattering words, and assuming an air of self-importance. "I am the ruler of the world. I am great and wise. No one will dare to resist me. I will exterminate the spirits of the superior kingdom."

The troops were gathered, and of each division the best individuals selected for making the first assault under the command of Clavo; but now a great difficulty presented itself at the very start; for even the common people among the gnomes had become so much accustomed to arguing, that not a soldier would obey an order without having all the "whys" and "wherefores" explained to him. Each private wanted to know why this or that order was given, and whether it would be advisable to follow it, and what it was intended for, and whether not perhaps something better might be done, and so forth. This caused an endless delay; because, for the purpose of obtaining the consent of the subordinates to follow an order, the commanding general had to explain his views and argue his points with the officers; the officers had to reason it out with the corporals, and they in their turn had to discuss it with the privates and obtain their consent. Some thought the given order practicable, others made objections and refused to obey, and nobody could be induced to act against his own views. From this state of affairs there arose a great deal of delay, difficulties, and waste of time; but at last the assault was made.

They were driven back with great loss, and others took their places, but with the same result. The most obstinate gnomes were sent forward, and for two nights lasted the battle, in which wonderful deeds of stubbornness and daring were accomplished, with no other effect than bringing destruction upon the gnomes and doing no harm to the fairies, whose stronghold was inaccessible; for whenever our soldiers rushed up through the tunnel, a single effusion of lightning was sufficient to kill the greater portion of them, while the rest were driven back mutilated and scorched.

Thus the flower of the kingdom of the gnomes was destroyed; the wails of the widows and orphans resounded, and the king wept unceasingly, beating the air with his arms in sheer despair and impotent fury. Nevertheless, owing to the persuasions of the princess, the gnomes would not desist. She made the king believe that, according to her theory about the exhaustion of energy, the lightning power of the fairies could not endure very long, and the king believed all she said.

                     The comet-drivers

"If we cannot go up to them," she said, "we must make them come down." To this end she instituted sham flights among the troops, hoping to induce the elfs to pursue them, and she tried all possible means for beguiling the inhabitants of the upper realm, and lead them into a trap. She made to them all kinds of false promises, but those spirits saw that her motive was not pure; she tried to attract them by her song, but her voice had become harsh and disagreeable, like the screeching of an owl.

In fact, I must confess it, although it may not be considered nice to speak ill of a lady, especially if she is one's intended wife, that Adalga had become somewhat disagreeable. This war brought out the worst traits of her character, and no means were too contemptible for her to employ, provided they held out a prospect to her for accomplishing what she desired.

It has already been stated that, at the time which corresponded to day in our world, the gnomes fell into a death-like sleep, from which they did not awaken until night settled upon the earth. Not being a gnome, I was not subject to the law of their nature, but could remain awake and observe what was taking place during their sleep.

Thus, during the third day after the beginning of the struggle, I was lying awake in the camp, while all the gnomes were asleep. I was watching the entrance of the tunnel, which appeared like a circular opening in the clouds, through which issued a faint light, when suddenly it became illumined by a roseate radiance of great beauty, somewhat like the aurora borealis or northern light. At the same time I heard a chant as of angel voices, and directly afterwards there issued from the tunnel a bevy of the most charming fairies, each representing a luminous living flower, with a beautiful face in its midst. There were Oleanders, Orange-Blossoms, Roses, Camelias, Anemones, Pansies, Forget-me-nots, Daffodils, etc., and out of the chalice or heart of each looked a childlike face, peaceful and smiling; but the greatest and most radiant of all was a white Lotus flower, in whose midst dwelt the fairy queen, with a crown of diamonds upon her head.

I was not at all alarmed. I saw—if I am permitted to use such an unscientific expression—that they intended no harm. It would have been useless to attempt to awaken the sleeping gnomes; I therefore remained still, and looked at the spirits of the flowers through my half-closed lids. They moved about among the sleepers, singing and scattering blossoms, and when they came to the place where Adalga slept, they drew around her in a circle, throwing flowers upon her, such beautiful ones as I had never seen before, and which did not fade away either, when they touched the ground; but the princess smiled in her sleep, as if she had a pleasant dream, and her features assumed an expression that made her look agreeable in spite of her ugliness.

The fairies stood regarding the sleeper with great attention, while pity and hope were expressed in their faces, and the Lotus flower stepped out of her chalice, and sang in a silvery voice a song in a language which I did not understand literally, but whose sentiments became clear to my heart, and might perhaps be expressed in the following lines:—

"We are the spirits of the voice of truth.

Symbols of beauty, harmony, and youth;

We teach thee wisdom from the sphere above,

If thou wilt listen to our song of love.

Without the darkness light cannot be known;

To know truth, falsehood must be overthrown.

Peace without effort would be death to thee;

Nought but the battle leads to victory.

Without a struggle there's no joy in rest;

Only through evil good can manifest.

The comet-drivers

Without the dust of earth no plant will grow,

And no one rise who never fell below.

Nought comes from nought, and no amount of toil

Will raise a fruit tree from a barren soil;

But the good seed within the hot-bed needs

No other help but rooting out the weeds.

Knowledge is power, but it serves you naught,

Unless you practise that which you were taught;

Toil without knowledge is a fruitless tree,

Science unused is naught but theory.

Knowledge is power, but remember well

You must yourself destroy the magic spell;

And Lucifer, who came but to redeem,

Redeems you only if you conquer him."

Thus the queen of the Lotus ended her song, and floated away with her companions. The last I saw of them was a roseate light shining from the mouth of the tunnel. I then fell asleep myself, and slept until I was awakened by the blowing of horns, the blast of trumpets, and beating of drums, calling the troops together for a renewal of the fight, and those who were so inclined got up and joined the ranks.

I went to the princess, and found her to be in a pensive mood, while her loquaciousness was less than usually active—a circumstance which I attributed to the visit of the fairies. I asked her whether she had experienced a pleasant dream.

"I do not believe in dreams," she answered. "Scientists never attribute any importance to dreams or to subjective experiences; our attention is fully engaged by the objective realities of life."

"Confound your false science!" I said. "It deals, after all, with nothing but appearances and dreams. The fairies seemed to me very objective."

"So you saw them?" replied Adalga. "Perhaps it was your thought-transfer which caused that hallucination."

"Let it be what it may," I said. "It is of little importance from what we receive a lesson; the lesson itself is that which we ought to consider."

"We are not in the habit of accepting lessons," she answered, "unless they come from some well-recognised authority."

To this I answered:

"Truth is truth, no matter by whom it is uttered."

"Prove it!" exclaimed the princess, and as I remained silent, she continued, sneeringly: "If we are asked to listen to a theory, the first thing is to inquire about the claims for credibility of him who puts them forth. Upon what authority does his assertion rest? What books can he quote for the support of his opinion? If all this is settled, we may listen to his proofs, and decide whether we will accept them or not."

I groaned. "Alas!" I said; "in your science it is all creed, but no perception of truth."

Off she went, and soon cries of distress were heard between the explosions that followed. The storming party was beaten back. A fresh attack was ordered, but the troops had become disheartened, and refused to enter the tunnel. Some, however, were inclined to proceed, and called the others cowards; and this led to a quarrel among the troops, which resulted in a fight, and the fight developed into an open revolt, during which it soon became plain that the mutineers were in great strength. In vain the king butted his head against everything that happened to come in his way, in vain the princess proved by irrefutable arguments that the loyal troops could not be conquered; they were beaten anyhow, and we were driven back with them in the direction of Lucifer's temple. Soon after that we were pressed so hard that we had to seek shelter behind the walls. Multitudes thronged in after us, and many more sought to enter, but could find no room. The space became so crowded that the gnomes pushed each other, and struggled for room. Thus they pressed against the pedestal of the queen frog, some climbing upon it, others trying to climb; and in the midst of the uproar the monster began to sway, and, losing its balance, it fell.

A crash followed. The frog was broken to pieces, and volumes of poisonous vapour coming from the phosphorus filled the place. Instinctively I closed my eyes, and when I opened them again the whole assembly of gnomes had become transformed into animals. Bimbam I. had turned into an ox, rushing madly through the crowd; in the place of the commanding general stood a sheep; and, to my horror, I beheld a big goat in the place of the princess. Cravatu had become a black lizard, with yellow spots, and all the rest of the gnomes now appeared in animal forms. There were bats flying about, mice rushing into holes, spiders crawling over the walls; and two ministers, having turned into brass beetles, were rolling a ball of dirt over the ground. Cats squalled, rats whistled, frogs croaked, sheep bleated, dogs yowled and barked, and the whole was in a terrible confusion.

The goat stared at me in an offensive manner, which I was bound to resent. So I said:

"You need not stare at me in this manner. Is this your gratitude for my conferring upon you the blessings of civilisation? Is this the thanks which I am to receive from you for teaching you logic, and how to draw inferences from postulates? To you we owe all this misfortune. It is your confounded curiosity that made you meddle with things for whose conception you were not mature, and which you could not realise, that brought about this war. The stubbornness with which you kept clinging to your preconceived opinions has caused this mutiny. Now you have turned into a goat, and I can only say it served you right."

The goat tried to speak, but brought forth only a stuttering "ma-a-a-h," which sounded to me like the ironical laughter of a scientist of old laughing at the rotundity of the earth.

The princess—that is to say, the goat—lowered her head.

"You need not get angry!" I exclaimed, feeling somewhat alarmed. "You ought to be ashamed of yourself. I wish that I had never seen you. I am only sorry that it is I who is to be married to a goat."

But before I had time to finish this sentence, the goat made a vicious rush at me, and gave me a butt on my stomach which took my breath. I grasped the princess by her horns, and a struggle ensued.

Just then I heard somebody yell in an unearthly manner, and recognised the voice as that of Professor Cracker. In a moment the situation became perfectly clear to me, and I was no longer Mulligan, but Mr Schneider. Jeremiah Stiffbone was close to me, calling upon somebody to have pity upon his soul; and from under him there came forth a series of indefinite grunts, in which I recognised Mr Scalawag's voice. The goat escaped, and I knew that we still were in that hole in the Untersberg, near the Dragon's Den, and that my adventure among the gnomes had been only a dream.

The rest may easily be imagined. The subterranean passage, into which we had entered for obtaining shelter, had another outlet upon the other side of the hill, and through that a herd of goats had come in for some purpose; but the rest of one of them had been rudely disturbed by the foot of Professor Cracker. No serious harm, however, was done, while the experience was not without scientific value, as it proved that the goat was very spirited—a circumstance that might be regarded as going to show that there was some spirit after all in that goat. This theory I, however, advance merely as a working hypothesis, leaving it to the reader to use his own judgment as to whether he will accept it as wholly true, or only in part.

Thus Mr Schneider's story ended, and nothing has been heard publicly of the gnomes ever since. It is even believed that they keep their doors locked against all reformers. But, in commemoration of the event described, a board has been put up in the Dragon's Den, upon which a representation of the encounter between the committee and the spirit of that goat has been roughly painted by an amateur artist; and below the picture there is a description of the adventure in doggerel verse, which caused me a great deal of trouble to translate, but which might be rendered in English as follows:—

"Stop, wanderer, and behold with silent contemplation,

How exact science fought interior revelation.

The cleverest thing that Cracker had invented

Was by a stupid goat, with her two horns resented.

Alas! such is the fate of all the would-be wise;

We only know for sure that which we realise."

THE END